PROTAGORAS

The Library of Liberal Arts
OSKAR PIEST, FOUNDER

PROTAGORAS

PLATO

Benjamin Jowett's translation, extensively revised by
MARTIN OSTWALD

Edited, with an introduction, by
GREGORY VLASTOS

• •

The Library of Liberal Arts

published by

THE BOBBS-MERRILL COMPANY, INC.

INDIANAPOLIS • NEW YORK

CONTENTS
· · · · · · · · · · · · · · · · ·

INTRODUCTION

PART ONE: PROTAGORAS

1. *The Man*

The well-born Hippocrates blushes when he has to admit that Protagoras would make a sophist out of him: [1] there is a social stain on this profession. There is danger in it, too: Protagoras speaks of "precautions" he has to take when he tells the world he is a sophist, and adds the hope that "by the favor of heaven no harm will come of the acknowledgment" (317bc). He must have been a man of exceptional gifts to steer his perilous course for forty years [2] up and down the Greek world not only unharmed, but one of the most successful self-made men of Greece. He earned more money from his profession than did "Pheidias and ten other sculptors," [3] and more than money. When Athens established her great Pan-Hellenic colony at Thurii in 443, the design of the city was entrusted to the foremost city-planner of his day, Hippodamus of Miletus; the no less important job of drafting its laws was given to Protagoras.[4] Only a man who enjoyed the personal friendship

[1] 312a. (This and similar references throughout the Introduction will be all to the *Protagoras*. The number refers to the Stephanus pages which are marked in all modern editions of Plato's text and in scholarly translations, including the present. The accompanying letters, a, b, c, d, or e, refer to subdivisions of the Stephanus page which are also marked in editions of the Greek text.)

[2] *Meno* 91e.

[3] *Meno* 91d.

[4] Heracleides of Pontus *ap.* Diogenes Laertius, *Lives of the Philosophers* 9.50. (This work will be referred to hereafter simply by its author's initials as "D.L.") Cf. V. Ehrenberg, "The Foundation of Thurii," *Amer. Journal of Philology* 69 (1948), pp. 168-69.

and admiration of Pericles,[5] and also the respect of most of
Greece, could have been assigned such a role in this showy
act of imperial réclame.

Plato, who tells us elsewhere of the sophist's "good repu-
tation, which to this day [a decade or more after his death] he
retains," [6] says nothing in this dialogue to damage it. For the
huckster of ideas (313cd) Plato, of course, has no use; and
when he makes Protagoras' Great Speech culminate in some
straightforward sales talk (328bc), he associates our sophist
very firmly with his base employment. But he also makes it
clear that, unlike some salesmen, this one has moral inhibi-
tions. Protagoras refuses to admit that injustice is compatible
with *sophrosynē*; [7] many would assert this, he says, but not
he: he would be ashamed to say such a thing. Again, he refuses to identify a life of pleasure with the good life; all he will
admit is that the pleasant life is good for one who "find[s]
pleasure in what is good and noble" (351c); and he adds that
he says this not just for the sake of argument, but "having regard also to the whole of [his] life" (351d). When he is worsted
in the argument, he does not turn to snide remarks, abuse,

---

[5] There is a story (Stesimbrotus *ap.* Plutarch, *Pericles* 36) of a daylong
discussion between Pericles and Protagoras.

[6] *Meno* 91e. This is said in a context where Socrates argues against
Anytus that if sophists did corrupt the young they would be found out, and
makes Protagoras his star example. I believe this is absolutely inconsistent
with stories of Protagoras' condemnation to exile or death for impiety (for
the sources see E. Derenne, *Les Procès d' Impiété*, Liége, 1930, p. 54, notes 3
and 4; it will be seen that the evidence is conflicting and none of it goes
back to fifth- or fourth-century sources), though perfectly consistent with a
prosecution by somebody or other (according to Aristotle, *ap.* D.L. 9.54,
Euathlus, probably the same man mentioned by comic poets—Derenne, *op.
cit.*, p. 50, n. 2—as a notorious sycophant); in a place like Athens a prosecu
tion would be no blot on one's record, and would be quite enough to give
rise to later tales of condemnation.

[7] 333c. This word is the translator's despair. Its original meaning is
something like 'having a healthy mind'; it can mean any or all of the following: discretion, prudence, reasonableness, decency, good sense, modera-
tion, temperance, self-control—the last of which has been favored in the
present translation of the dialogue.

ridicule, or threats.[8] At the end he has the good grace to congratulate his opponent. "I admire you," he tells Socrates, "above all the men I meet, and far above all men of your age; I would not be surprised if you were to become one of those who are distinguished for their wisdom." [9] The magnanimity of these remarks is self-conscious, but not insincere. He has lost a battle but not his poise, and bears the victor no grudge.

2. The Great Speech (320c-328d)

The "Myth" with which the Speech begins is simply a figurative representation of Protagoras' speculations about the origins of civilization.[10] Stripped of its traditional imagery,[11]

---

[8] To get some perspective on Protagoras compare the reactions of some of Socrates' trounced opponents in other dialogues: Thrasymachus in *Rep.* 350de, 352b, 354a; Callicles in *Gorg.* 505cd, 511a, 515e, and, most of all, the veiled threat at 521c; Hippias at *Hp. Ma.* 304ab and *Hp. Mi.* 373b.

[9] The reader should be warned that I do not always follow exactly the Jowett-Ostwald translation of the text.

[10] Presented in his book, "On the Primitive State (of Human Affairs)." For our Myth as a source for the teachings of this book see especially W. Nestle, *Vom Mythos zum Logos*, Stuttgart, 1942, pp. 282-289.

[11] This imagery must be constantly borne in mind, else parts of the Myth will be misunderstood, particularly the account of religion as a human invention. Since the reference to "man's share in divinity" (and also the further remark of man's "kinship with the deity," though this may not have been in the original text) is inconsistent with Protagoras' known agnosticism about the existence of the gods (H. Diels and W. Kranz, *Fragmente der Vorsokratiker*, 6th ed., Berlin, 1952, 80 B 4; Plato, *Tht.* 162e), it has been supposed (e.g. Cherniss, *Amer. Journal of Philology* 71 (1950), p. 87; P. Friedländer, *Platon*, I, 2nd ed., Berlin, 1954, p. 346) that this part of the account can only express the views of Plato, not those of Protagoras. This supposition becomes unnecessary if we reckon these sentiments as parts of the mythical apparatus. Man's share in "the divine lot" is surely his participation in the *arts* which are represented in this very Myth (as in Herodotus 2.53.2, with which cf. Hesiod, *Theog.* vv. 73-74, 203-04) as originally belonging to the gods: the mechanical arts to Hephaestus and Athena, the political art to Zeus ("in his keeping," 321d). The temporal priority assigned to the invention of religion is also to be understood as mythical (a handsome compliment to the divine "givers" of all the arts): Protagoras was

a it has two main theses: first, that the arts are the human counterpart to the various devices which insure the survival of animal species; unlike theirs, man's survival weapons are, as we would say, cultural, or, as Protagoras speaks of them, matters of art (*technē*) or knowledge (*epistēmē, sophia*): they have to be invented at the beginning, and then transmitted by some sort of learning and teaching. *b* Secondly, that the "political" art is a no less authentic feature of this cultural equipment than the "industrial" ones, no less necessary for survival: men could not have won the struggle against nature ("the war against the brutes," 322b) unless they had learned how to live with one another.

These are powerful ideas that could be used for many purposes. Protagoras' immediate use for them is polemical. Socrates has turned the gathering into a debate on the problem "Can Virtue be Taught?" Protagoras is not content just to defend the affirmative. He goes over to the offensive, following up his reply, 'Yes, it can be taught' with 'to all by all.' [12] Let us give him a chance to explain what he is trying to do, and how:

'Don't think this *to all by all* a defiant flourish. No, it is the very thing needed to clarify the problem. Socrates' argument rests on a hidden assumption: if virtue could be taught, it would be taught to a few and by a few. Grant this hypothetical, and the antecedent will look false, for the consequent is certainly false. To solve the difficulty [13] I must show you that the hypothetical itself is false. This I can easily do, beginning with the anthropological teachings you've just heard. These have explained to you that what Socrates and I call *virtue*—the sum of right dealings in human [14] relations,

---

not such a fool as to suppose men could have religious beliefs and a cult before they had either language or piety (which is part of the "political art," 323e, 325a).

[12] I use the double quotes, ". . . ," for direct quotations; the single quotes here call attention to the fact that no direct quotation is involved.

[13] Or "perplexity," 324e.

[14] Protagoras assumes without argument that the very same things

justice, piety, *sophrosynē,* and the rest [15]—is a necessity of social existence. From this it follows that *every* member of society must have virtue. And if everyone is to have it, everyone must learn it, for how else could an art be acquired? [16] To this I add: and everyone must be able to teach it. This I can prove independently of my theory of cultural origins, by having you look at everyday facts and helping you to understand their meaning. Think of what happens when we praise or blame. We don't do it with the intention to teach. But aren't we teaching just the same? When we express approval of this, disapproval of that, aren't we as much as saying, Do this, don't do that? Similarly, when we punish, if we do it rationally, we are surely not just venting our rage for what has been done and can't be undone, but teaching a good lesson to the offender himself and other people.[17] In these two ways, not to speak of others, all of us are moral instructors. Once you have seen this, you will not be puzzled by the things Socrates has brought up,[18] and you will now see why you were puzzled earlier. Just think how puzzling the learning of your native tongue would be if you assumed that if Greek could be taught it would be taught only by a few and to a few.' [19]

---

make up "political virtue" (323a) and "human virtue" (325a)—an assumption which Socrates would be the last to question.

[15] The first three are the only ones mentioned after the Myth (323a, 323e–324a, 325a), and Socrates who stores this triad carefully in his mind (329c), makes a special point of the later addition of wisdom and courage to the list (330a); but he is unnecessarily fussy, for Protagoras never said that the first triad are the only virtues.

[16] That moral qualities are learned is confirmed by the forthcoming arguments that they are taught, since 'X is taught to Y' implies 'Y learns X.'

[17] Protagoras is apparently the first Western thinker who formally repudiated the vindictive and retributory, in favor of the deterrent and reformatory, views of punishment.

[18] 319b–320b. Their specific rebuttal by Protagoras can be easily made out, and needs no special comment here.

[19] For a discussion of the Great Speech which clears up some common misunderstandings of its doctrine, see G. B. Kerferd, "Protagoras' Doctrine of Justice and Virtue in the PROTAGORAS," *Journal of Hellenic Studies* 73 (1953), pp. 42–45.

3. *Protagorean Subjectivism*

Protagoras is past fifty at the dramatic date of our dialogue,[20] and we may be reasonably certain that well before this time he had written the famous essay, "Truth," [21] whose opening sentence ran—

> Of all things the measure is man: both of things that are [22] (man is the measure) that they are, and of things that are not (man is the measure) that they are not.

I hazard a reconstruction of the sense of this extremely obscure sentence. I put it in the form of a dialogue which pieces together almost all the scraps of information about Protagoras' subjectivist philosophy which come to us from sources other than our dialogue: [23]

——What "man" are you talking about?

Protagoras. Every man, you, me, anybody.

——Even men who haven't studied science or philosophy?

Prot. Aren't they men? [24]

[20] "There is no one here present of whom I might not be the father," 317c; he is, at the very least, fifteen years older than Socrates, who was born at 470 B.C. and would be in his middle or late thirties at the dramatic date of the dialogue, "which cannot be put later than 433," A. E. Taylor, *Plato*, London, 1949, p. 236.

[21] Our authority for the title is Plato, *Tht.* 161c. "Throwers," listed by Diels-Kranz as an alternative title, is due to a much later authority (Sextus, *Adv. Math.* 7.60), and is more likely to have been originally a descriptive term (because of the 'downing' or 'throwing'—an image drawn from wrestling—of traditional philosophical doctrines in this essay). Of its date we have no evidence; but the extremely radical ideas it contains are most likely those of a younger man.

[22] Literally, "of beings" or "realities."

[23] The main sources of my account are: Plato, *Crat.* 385c–386e; *Tht.* 152a–c, 166c–168b, 169d–172b; *Euthyd.* 285e–286d (with which cf. *Tht.* 167ab, *Crat.* 429d); Arist., *Met.* 998a2–4, D.L. 9.50–56.

[24] For the importance of this point see E. Kapp in *Gnomon* 12 (1936), pp. 70ff., or the excellent account of Kapp's views in von Fritz, "*Nous, Noein,* etc.," *Classical Philology* 41 (1946), p. 22. The essential point is that for Protagoras' great predecessors (Heraclitus, Parmenides) and contemporaries (Empedocles, Anaxagoras) "men" or "mortals" and their "opinions"

—But these men go by appearances; they haven't the sense to distinguish appearance from reality.

Prot. And they are perfectly right. Appearance *is* reality.[25] Even what you philosophers call "reality" is just what appears true to them.

—But appearances are not consistent. The same wind often feels warm to me, cold to you.

Prot. Then it *is* warm for you, cold for me.[26]

—But what is it in itself?

Prot. "Wind-in-itself"? I know of no such thing.[26a] Do you?

---

stand for error and delusion in contrast to the "being," "reality," or "truth" of the philosophers. For Protagoras "opinions" or "appearances," hitherto scorned by philosophy, become the measure of "being" or "truth."

[25] The reader should bear in mind features of the Greek which lent some plausibility to this extraordinary doctrine: the word for 'appears' (*phainetai*) need not be used in the pejorative sense of 'seems,' but may still be used in its original sense of 'comes to light' or 'is manifest': the term for 'opinion' (*doxa*) can cover all kinds of mental processes, ranging from fantasy, through sense perception, to intellectual judgment and decision.

[26] Plato, *Tht.* 152b.

[26a] Here I depart from the widely held view that, according to Protagoras, "the various and conflicting characteristics perceived by men all exist objectively as material parts of the perceived object," H. Cherniss, *Aristotle's Criticism of Pre-Socratic Philosophy*, Baltimore, 1935, p. 369; cf. also V. Brochard, *Etudes de Philosophie Ancienne*, Paris, 1912, Chapter III; E. Zeller, *History of Greek Philosophy*, Engl. trans. by S. F. Alleyne, vol. II, London, 1881, pp. 446ff.; H. Gomperz, *Sophistik und Rhetorik*, Leipzig, 1912, p. 231ff.; M. Untersteiner, *The Sophists*, Engl. transl. by K. Freeman, Oxford, 1954, pp. 43ff.; and Kerferd, listed at note 46, below. Since Brochard's brilliant defense of this "objectivist" interpretation ("O") in 1889, much of the supporting evidence has rotted away, for it is now agreed that the "secret doctrine of Protagoras" ("SDP") at *Tht.* 152d ff. is Plato's own invention. The only remaining evidence worth talking about is that of Sextus, *Pyrrh. Hyp.* 1. 216–219, and Aristotle, *Met.* 1007b 18ff., 1047a 4ff., 1062b 13ff. But Sextus swallowed SDP (cf. H. Maier, *Sokrates,* Tübingen, 1913, p. 208, n. 3), and his crucial statement, "he says that the reasons for all appearances subsist in matter, matter being in itself potentially all that it appears to all" (218; cf. 219 *sub fin.*) is very probably what *he* made of SDP and is, in any case, glaringly late in thought and idiom: Aristotelian potentiality of the material substrata, baptized "*logoi* of appearances" in a Stoic font, is fathered on the first of the sophists. In Aris-

The only wind you can know is the one you can feel: this is the wind-for-you, and you are its measure.

——If that is the way you reason, you might as well hold that all beliefs are true.

Prot. I do. All beliefs *are* true for those who believe them.[27]

——But that is fantastic.

Prot. I can prove that no such thing as a false belief can exist. Suppose it did, it would have to be about something or about nothing. It couldn't be about nothing: you can't even think of nothing. So it must be about something—something

---

totle's testimony we can see that O is not a report, but a constructive inference: "he said that man is the measure of all things, *meaning nothing but* that what anyone believes stably exists; *this being so, it follows that* the same thing both is and is not, is both good and evil . . . , *because* often this thing appears noble to some, its opposite to others," *Met.* 1062b 13–18. What Aristotle's inference is worth may be judged from the omission of "for him" after "stably (!) exists" and in the next sentence: cf. note 27, below. The same blunder in Sextus ("all things which appear to men exist"), who, however, goes on, "while those which appear to no man do not exist," totally unaware of the contradiction between *this* and what he said a moment ago (and repeats in the very next sentence) about the "*logoi* of appearances" (cf. also *Adv. Math.* 7. 64: Protagoras "left nothing either existing in itself or false"). Testimony so confused and corrupt cannot justify us in imputing to Protagoras a view which would be so out of line with his well-authenticated doctrines (notes 27, 28, below) that all beliefs are true, and that false belief is impossible.

27 *Tht.* 170a, "that which is believed by anyone is (true) for him who believes it"—an unusually reliable statement of Protagorean doctrine, for it occurs in a context (169e–170a) where Plato carefully discriminates between admissions *he* has been putting into Protagoras' mouth (with consequent doubt whether Protagoras himself would have made them) and one which comes "from his (Protagoras') own statement." It will be noticed that in my little dialogue Protagoras is very fussy about adding "for . . ." after "true" or "is" or "real," while his thickheaded interlocutor keeps ignoring the difference. Even Plato himself is not as careful as he should be on this point. While he puts in the "for . . ." almost invariably while *reporting* or *describing* Protagoras' doctrine (not only at 170a, but at 152b, c, 158a, and all through 166c–167c, where the repetition gets almost tiresome, and then again at 171e–172a; also at *Crat.* 385e–386d), he sometimes drops it in the course of *arguing* against Protagoras (e.g. in the "exquisite" argument at 171a), thereby inadvertently vitiating his own polemic.

real for you, else why should you be thinking about it? And if your belief is about something real for you, how can it be false for you? [28]

——Nonsense. There are millions of false beliefs.

Prot. Mention one that is false for him who believes it.

——Will you accept an example from geometry?

Prot. Gladly.

——Tell the man in the street that a tangent touches a circle at just one point, and he'll swear you are wrong. Would you say his belief is true?

Prot. True for him. The only tangent for him is the one he can see; and you are not going to tell me that he can *see* a tangent that touches a circle at just one point? [29]

——I suppose you have no scruples about applying your appearance-is-reality doctrine to morals.

Prot. Are you insinuating there is something unscrupulous about that? I am in most respectable company here. Herodo-

[28] I am only slightly expanding here a sentence which occurs in Plato's own 'defense for Protagoras': "For it is neither possible to think [or 'believe' (*doxasai*)] things that are not, nor (is it possible to think) things other than those one feels, and these are always true," *Tht.* 167a7–b1. and cf. 167d2. The impossibility of false statements (and, consequently, of false beliefs) is independently attested for "those about Protagoras" at *Euthyd.* 286c.

[29] All our evidence on this point consists of a passing allusion in Aristotle (*Met.* 998a 2–4): "for a [sensible] circle touches a straightedge not at one point only, but in the way Protagoras said it did, refuting the mathematicians." This has been taken to mean (most recently by T. Heath, *Mathematics in Aristotle,* Oxford, 1949, pp. 204–05) that (a) Aristotle understood Protagoras to argue against the mathematicians that their doctrine was false for everyone, and the general inference has been that (b) Protagoras denied that the orthodox doctrine of the tangent was even true for mathematicians. The possibility has been ignored that (c) Protagoras only argued that the mathematical doctrine was not true for everyone (i.e., not true for the man in the street, who thought it false, though true enough for mathematicians, who thought it true). From the citation it is not even clear that (a) is true; and even if it were, (b) would not follow: Aristotle could easily have missed the difference between "false for everyone" and "not true for everyone." (c) is in line, much more than (b), with the general trend of Protagoras' thought.

tus,[30] you will recall, said Cambyses was mad because he despised the burial customs of other people. All I am doing is to generalize the notion our historian has applied to something as sacrosanct as funeral rites, and say that anything held right and just in a given state is right and just for it.[31]

4. *How Agreement is Secured*

None of the doctrines of this dialogue are mentioned in the Great Speech.[32] Is this strange? Plato arranges things so that it will not seem so. He puts Protagoras into a tight spot, with no room for the exhibition of his dazzling paradoxes. Socrates slips in between the sophist and his admiring audience, precipitates a debate, fixes its topic, throws up swiftly a case for it, and leaves Protagoras no alternative but to fight on Socrates' own terrain. But why did Plato arrange things in this way? Because Socrates is the hero of this drama, and his interests dictate the choice of subject matter.[33] In Protagoras' *ontological* subjectivism—in the "appearance-is-reality" doctrine asserted with unrestricted generality, 'everything is for any given person such as it appears to that person'—Socrates would be interested no more than in any of the great ontologies and cosmologies which crowded the intellectual landscape of his time.[34] In Protagoras'

[30] 3.38.1; cf. Pindar, frag. 215. Cf. F. Heinimann, *Physis und Nomos* (Basel, 1945), pp. 78ff., who thinks Herodotus was directly influenced by Protagoras at this point; but the evidence is inconclusive.

[31] *Tht.* 167c; 172b.

[32] Nor, for that matter, later on in the dialogue. The only thing that looks like a piece of genuine Protagorean theorizing is at 334a–c, which has been generally recognized as one of the arguments Protagoras used to support moral relativism. Here it is used only to help the sophist out of a fix in the argument, and he has no chance to make clear its connection with his other doctrines.

[33] An even more striking instance is the *Gorgias,* where the philosophical doctrines of the illustrious sophist are ignored even more completely than those of Protagoras in our dialogue.

[34] That Socrates was familiar with all these doctrines goes without saying; so would be most of the audience in the house of Callias. This is an

moral subjectivism—for the doctrine that goodness, justice, piety, and the like, are for each such as they appear to each— Socrates would have the keenest interest. The two doctrines are logically distinct. Though the first implies the second, the second by no means implies the first, is by far the stronger, more defensible of the two, and must have been then, as it is now, an influential position, held by many who would not dream of saddling themselves with the freakish extremism of Protagoras' generalized subjectivism. Under such circumstances the best way to indulge Socrates' interests would be to steer the discussion firmly away from Protagoras' ontology, keep entirely to his moral doctrine, and deal with the subjectivist assumptions of the latter only by indirection: to bring them up directly would require references to the formulae of "Truth," where man-is-the-measure and appearance-is-reality were applied promiscuously to sensible qualities, mathematical truths, and who knows what else in addition to moral concepts, and thus bring up the very things Socrates would wish to exclude from the discussion.[35] Moral subjectivism then must be assumed by Protagoras and refuted by Socrates without being mentioned by either. Such seems to be the order Plato set himself in this dialogue. For the refutation one must look to the climax of the debate,

---

age in which the books of Anaxagoras (the most difficult of the cosmologists) sell for no more than a drachma at Athens (*Apol.* 26d, with Burnet's note *ad loc.*). When Socrates speaks of cosmological doctrines as ". . . things of which I know nothing, great or small" (*Ap.* 19c), he only means that he can't tell whether or not they are true. To the ontological doctrine of Protagoras (judging from the tone of *Euthyd.* 286c) Socrates would not even give the benefit of such doubt; he would feel that it rested on sophistries, but was not important enough to be worth refuting. Plato, unlike his teacher, did feel it worth refuting, and he gave Socrates the job in the *Theaetetus,* but only after he had made of Socrates a mouthpiece for his own views.

35 It is worth remembering that the dearth of philosophical terminology (no words for "subjectivism," "relativism," "ontology," "epistemology") would make it more difficult to identify doctrines Socrates would like to exclude from a discussion without actually *stating* them and, in a live discussion, also explaining them to some degree, thus defeating Plato's dramatic purpose.

the place at which Socrates extracts the admission he will use to destroy Protagoras in the last round of the debate. This is what happens at 356de, when Protagoras is forced to concede that "the saving principle of life" is not "the power of appearance," but the "art of measurement": what can this "power of appearance" be but an indirect reference to the appearance-is-reality doctrine in its bearing on the good life? [36] But all this lies much further ahead. We are still in the Great Speech, and what we must look for here is some link between the unnamed moral subjectivism of his position and the explicit content of the Speech.[37]

I can best exhibit this link by resuming the dialogue where it broke off in the preceding section:

——But there is often disagreement *within* a state. Is the minority view wrong when it conflicts with the official doctrine?

Prot. Not wrong for the minority.

——So you would require the minority to act in ways that seem unjust to them, and are unjust for them?

Prot. I see no logical inconsistency about that, but if you mean that it would be very awkward, I quite agree. When people differ in their moral judgments, it is very hard for them to avoid acting out their disagreements, and then the very purpose for which morality was invented—to facilitate friendly and harmonious social relations [38]—would be defeated. This is a prac-

[36] An allusion which often passes unnoticed by the commentators; but see W. Nestle, in his edition of the *Protagoras,* with introduction and commentary (Leipzig, 1931), p. 48.

[37] I am arguing for an even closer link than has been assumed, e.g., by Taylor, *op. cit.,* p. 246, who sees that Protagoras' "whole argument depends on simply identifying 'goodness' with the actual traditions of an existing, civilized state," but not how the process of "teaching" described here would meet the problem of moral disagreement so far as it can be met on purely subjectivist assumptions. But one must take care not to overstate the connection. The "teaching" described in the Great Speech does not commit one to subjectivism (on almost any theory there would be some use for all of these processes) unless one adds the assumption (here tacit) that this is all there can be to moral teaching.

[38] 322c.

tical problem, and it calls for a practical answer. On my view moral disagreement is like a disease. You don't argue about it. You cure it.[39]

—How do you propose to do that?

Prot. The way it is done in every civilized community. Just think how many of the things you do are concerned with the *prevention* of disagreement in the first place, and then, if this fails, with its *cure.* You start with the child, telling him, "This is just, that is unjust . . . ; do this, don't do that," [40] and if he goes along with you the problem has been forestalled. If not, then, "like a bent and warped wood," you "straighten it by threats and blows." [41]

—By "straightening" it, you mean bring it into line with the mores of its elders?

Prot. What else? Or are you hankering after some straight-in-itself?

—But isn't what the little rebel thinks straight, straight for him?

Prot. Certainly. But you are missing the point. The point is not, who is right—the child or his parents? There is no sense to that question: there never is, in any case of moral disagreement. The only question that makes sense is how to get rid of the disagreement. And the answer to this is obvious. The parents can straighten the child according to their views, while the child is in no position to impose his on them.

There is no reason to prolong the dialogue. All the ways by which morality is "taught" according to the Great Speech are just so many variants for the indoctrination or 'conditioning' that has its start in infancy, as schoolteachers, lyre-masters, athletic coaches, lawmakers, law-enforcing agents, and all the ubiquitous agents of the established morality come to first share and then replace the original role of the parents. Protagoras, if he had time, might have enlarged the list of preventive measures

39 I extend the metaphor implied by "incurable" at 325ab.
40 325d.
41 *Loc. cit.*

and told us more of the lyre-master's way of charming the mind into conformity—the temples and statues, religious festivals and processions, speeches on state occasions, tragedy and comedy on the public stage, functions, so lavishly supported by the Periclean splendor-state, through which a civilized community keeps its hold on the heart and imagination of the citizen, ensuring that he will love what the city loves and hate what it hates.

5. The Role of the Wise Man

Imagine now a man who can, from time to time, resist and reverse these community pressures; when his appearances [42] disagree with the majority's, he may be able to bring them round to his. There is nothing in the theory to rule this out as a perfectly good way of resolving a disagreement. Whether the one "straightens" the many, or the many the one, it is all the same for the theory, so long as congruence results. But what are one man's chances of prevailing against the many? Protagoras would not believe them to be always hopeless, for he thinks of the majority as suggestible, manipulable, thoughtless: "As for the people, they have no understanding, and only repeat what their leaders tell them," [43] is one of his first remarks to Socrates. And later on in the dialogue: "But why, Socrates, need we investigate the opinion of the many, who just say anything that comes to their head?" [44] Are such remarks surprising in the mouth of a man who believes that the people are not only learners, but *teachers* of virtue? No. Nothing in the process described in the Great Speech requires either learner or teacher to

[42] Here and hereafter I use 'his appearances' as a convenient abbreviation for 'the way things appear to him.'

[43] 317a.

[44] 353a. It can scarcely be an accident that both of these are offhand remarks. I think Plato is suggesting that this man who was so anxious to justify the practices of democracy and was, in turn, rewarded with a commission like that of Thurii (note 4, above), had no respect for the people's intelligence, and gave it away when he was off his guard, as he never would in a book or formal speech.

think for oneself, or even to think: to weigh evidence, analyze concepts, examine reasons. Repeating whatever one's leaders tell one is a perfectly good way of teaching, on this view of teaching. Why then should Protagoras feel superior to these parroting multitudes? Simply because he *is* superior in ability to resolve moral disagreement in his favor; he is so much more adept in rubbing his own appearances into the minds of other people, instead of having theirs rub off on his.

Is this what makes him "wiser" than the rest? We must be careful here; it is so easy to overstate the point. It is best to stick closely to Protagoras' own example: [45] What makes the doctor "wise"? Certainly not the fact that his appearances are true (e.g., the sweetness of honey) while those of his patient's (to whose fevered palate honey tastes bitter) are false. For each of them, doctor and patient alike, honey is exactly what it appears: sweet for one, bitter for the other. The doctor is "wise" for the very different reason that he can *change* the patient, so that honey no longer tastes bitter to him, and not only this, but many other things which appear bad to him and are bad for him— the nausea, aches, general sense of weariness, etc.—vanish: the patient comes to feel well, and is well. The ability to work this kind of change is the way Protagorean "wisdom" must have been defined, and so it is in Plato's formulation of it in his 'defense for Protagoras': "By a 'wise' man I mean one who can change any of us to whom evil things appear and for whom evil things exist and make good things appear (to him) and exist (for him)." [46] Note that the definition is not

1. 'Wise' = 'has power to change men so that their appearances agree with his'

45 *Tht.* 166d–167c. There is no good reason to doubt that the comparison of the sophist-orator with the physician, which occurs in Plato's 'defense for Protagoras' was drawn from Protagoras' own writings. We find it also in Gorgias' *Helena* (14).

46 *Tht.* 166d. Kerferd, "Plato's Account of the Relativism of Protagoras," *Durham University Journal* (1949), p. 24, n. 27, objects to making "any of us" the object of "change" here. But that is what the sense calls for. The doctor changes the patient, not the honey.

but

    2. 'Wise' = 'has power to change men so that the result ap-
        pears good to them.' [47]

1 would be logically simpler; why then bring in the further
complication involved in *2*? One good reason would be the following: Even if *1* were correct, *2* would be the "wiser" way to
define "wise." A man who bases his claim to wisdom on his
mere ability to impose his thoughts on others is much less likely
to succeed in this very object than one who bases it on his ability to change their views in such a way that the result will be for
their own good—their good as judged by themselves and by
whatever norms are acceptable to themselves. A doctor who
does not undertake to do his best to make his patients feel well,
and says his job is just to make their feelings agree with his, is
not likely to have any patients. Nor would a sophist or politi-
cian succeed in fifth-century Greece, where power and influence
could only be reached by winning and keeping the public's
favor. But there is no reason to assume that this line of thinking
was Protagoras' only ground for preferring *2,* or that it was even
a consciously calculated reason. It is quite in line with the character with which Plato credits him that he should define "wisdom"—his own, that of his pupils, of his friend Pericles, and of
other distinguished orator-statesmen—in the benign terms of *2*:
power wielded over others to secure for them what they themselves feel to be good.

[47] Some scholars think Protagoras could, and did, assume, thirdly,
'Wise' = 'has power to substitute better beliefs for worse ones,' where 'better'
would be defined as "most in accordance with those of the man in a normal
condition of body and mind" (Burnet, *Greek Philosophy*, London, 1914, p.
116; so also Nestle, *Vom Mythos zum Logos*, Stuttgart, 1942, p. 276) or as
"more useful" (Kerferd, *op. cit.*, p. 25). This would imply that Protagoras
drops his subjectivism when he gets to this point; and only decisive evidence
that Protagoras made this enormous change could convince us that he did.
Our only relevant evidence (Plato's at *Tht.* 166d ff.) says no such thing;
when it is most formal and explicit, as in the above-cited definition of
"wise" at 166d, the terms "good" and "bad" are accompanied by the subjectivist signature, the coupling of "appears" with "is," which makes it
clear that the "good" and "evil" spoken of here are simply those which so
appear to the person for whom they exist.

The sophist Plato puts before us in our dialogue promises to fulfill and overfulfill this ideal of "wisdom." "Young man," he tells Hippocrates, "if you associate with me, on the very first day you will return home a better man than you came . . . and better every day than you were on the day before." [48] Not all sophists made such promises. Gorgias was satisfied to make his pupils better talkers, and thought this claim of making other people better a good joke.[49] But what does Protagoras mean by "better"—or does he mean anything at all? By his own subjectivist views this could mean all things to all men, leaving plenty of room for the might-is-right philosophy of Thrasymachus,[50] Callicles,[51] and the Athenian envoys in the Melian dialogue.[52] Protagoras' moral standards differ as much from these as white from black; they are the ideals of Athenian and Greek morality at its best: justice, *sophrosynē*, piety. If he differs from the tradition it is only to humanize it further—not brutalize it, like Callicles, whose "justice," a name for the unlimited right of the strong to take advantage of the weak, is modeled on what prevails "both among other animals and men . . ." [53] Protagoras stands by the old Hesiodic conviction that justice is what distinguishes men from animals.[54] God-sent for Hesiod, man-made for Protagoras, for both justice is joined with *aidos*,[55] sensitiveness to the feelings of others, respect for the rights of the weak, regard for the common good. Protagoras means to hold up this kind of justice before Hippocrates. It is enshrined in the moral beliefs of the young man's own com-

48 318a.
49 *Meno* 95c; cf. *Gorg.* 449a, where Gorgias says that his art is simply "rhetoric."
50 Plato, *Rep.* 338c ff.
51 *Gorg.* 483a ff.
52 Thucydides 5.89. 105.
53 *Gorg.* 483d. Cf. D. Loenen, *Protagoras and the Greek Community*, Amsterdam, 1940, p. 69.
54 Hesiod, *Works and Days* vv. 276–280, and cf. T. A. Sinclair, *History of Greek Political Thought*, London, 1951, p. 57.
55 The association of justice with *aidos* in Protagoras' Myth recalls Hesiod's *Aidos kai Nemesis*, v. 200, where *Nemesis* = Dikē (cf. *dikē* . . . *aidos* at v. 192).

munity, and its influence has been at work on him ever since the
never-ending prescription, "this is just, that unjust . . . ; do this,
don't do that," began in infancy. Protagoras' great persuasive
powers—Socrates likens them to the hypnotic spell of Orpheus'
voice[56]—will carry the molding of Hippocrates' soul in the
forms of justice, piety, *sophrosynē* to the last point of perfec-
tion to which the craft of a master molder can bring it. Could
a good and reasonable man have any fault to find with one who
promises to do this? Could Socrates?

PART TWO: SOCRATES

1. *The Man*

He is not a wholly attractive figure in this dialogue. His
irony, so impish in the *Hippias Major*, breath-taking in its ef-
frontery in the *Hippias Minor*, somber, even bitter, yet under
perfect control, in the *Euthyphro*, seems clumsy, heavy-handed
here. His fulsome compliments to Protagoras, continued after
they have lost all semblance of plausibility, become a bore. In
his exegesis of the poet [1] he turns into a practical joker, almost
a clown. He is entitled to his opinion that looking to poets for
moral instruction is like getting your music from the clever
harlots who dance and play the flute for the stupid bourgeois.[2]
But why act out this dubious metaphor in a labored one-
man charade, throwing in some philosophical edification on the
side, as when he drags in (by a misplaced comma) his doctrine
that no man sins voluntarily? [3] And his handling of Protagoras
is merciless, if not cruel. The steel-trap quality of his arguing
might be excused by the infinite importance he attaches to his
method and its results. It is not heartless, but just, that he
should not be deflected from his objective by any of the soph-

[56] 315ab, 328d.

[1] For an excellent discussion of this part of the dialogue see Woodbury's article, listed in the Bibliography.

[2] 347cd.

[3] 347d ff.

ist's diversionary moves. But when the job is done and the mortal stab has been delivered, is it necessary to make the victim himself give one more twist to the knife? [4]

Only a fine artist could worship a man, yet show him life-size, and with no crookedness of feature, no wart or wrinkle, smoothed out of the portrait. Only one conscious of his own reserves of power could be content to release this early study which records some of the tiresome things in Socrates without fully revealing what made him "of all the men of his time the best, the wisest, and most just," [5] and to those who knew him as lovable as he was disturbing. There will be time for that in the *Apology,* the *Crito,* and the *Gorgias,* time to show what manner of man this was of whom Alcibiades was to say:

> When I listen to him my heart leaps up much more than in a corybantic dance, his words move me to tears. I see this happen to many others too. When I listened to Pericles and other fine orators, I thought: They speak well. But nothing like this happened to me, my soul was not thrown into turmoil, I was not enraged at myself for living so like a slave. But this Marsyas has often put me into a state where I felt the life I lived was not worth living . . . He is the only man who ever made me feel ashamed.[6]

In just one place in this dialogue we get an inkling of a Socrates who could have been this to an Alcibiades—in that first scene with Hippocrates, when he talks to the young man with grave gentleness, like a father:

> I wonder whether you know what you are doing. . . . You are going to commit your soul to the care of a man you call a sophist. And yet I hardly think you know what a sophist is. . . . Are you aware of the danger you are running? . . . Watch out, my friend, don't take risks, don't gamble, with the most precious thing you have. . . .[7]

---

[4] My sympathies are wholly with Protagoras when he replies, "It is contentious of you, Socrates, to make me answer. Very well, then, I will gratify you, and say . . . ," 360e.

[5] The last words of the *Phaedo.*

[6] *Symp.* 215e, 216b.

[7] 312bc; 313a; 313e.

But the next moment he has climbed the public stage, or rather the ring he chooses to make of it, where all we shall soon see of him will be the prize fighter.[8] It is only between rounds that he looks up to his opponent as to a friend, and explains himself: "Do not imagine, Protagoras, that I have any other interest in asking questions of you but that of clearing up my own problems as they arise." [9] But the confession is immediately smothered in irony, and he does not resume it until the very end, when he tells his beaten opponent that "Promethean care for (his) whole life" is what drives him to these arguments.[10] The sincerity of the remark must have got across to Protagoras and helped elicit his rancorless reply.

[*Reproduce*

2. His Method

He puts a question to you, '*P* or not-*P*?' You say, '*P*.' —'But doesn't *P* imply *Q*?' —'Yes.' —'And *Q*, of course, implies *R*?' — 'To be sure.' —'But earlier you said, *S*, didn't you? Or is my memory at fault?' —'I did say *S*. And why not? Anything wrong with *S*?' —'Nothing in the world. Only, doesn't *S* imply *T*?' —'I suppose it does.' —'Do you only suppose? Aren't you sure?' — 'Yes, I am sure.' —'But now put *T* and *R* together. Are they consistent?' —'No.' —'*T* contradicts *R*, doesn't it?' —'It does.'— 'So if *T* is true, *R* must be false?' —'It must.' —'And since you agreed that *R* follows from *P*, then if *R* is false *P* must be false.' —'It must.' —'So *P* and *S* can't both be true. Which will you have?' Usually there is not much doubt about the answer. *P* was very plausible at first. But you feel so much more certain about *S* that if one of the two must go, you have no hesitation in sacrificing *P*.

The skeleton of the argument would be:

$$P \to Q \to R$$
$$S \to T$$

[8] The figure is Socrates' own, 339e.
[9] 348c. Cf. *Charm.* 166cd.
[10] 361d.

$T \to$ not-R
But not-$R \to$ not-$Q \to$ not-P.
Therefore, $T \to$ not-P.
Therefore, $S \to$ not-P.
(And S is true.
Therefore, P is false.)

This is the sort of thing that happens in Socratic arguments. Their form varies greatly: no two of them in our dialogue follow exactly the same logical pattern. But in one respect they are the same. The contradictory of some proposition, P—almost invariably one which seems true at first sight and is pronounced 'true' right off by the interlocutor—is deduced from one or more propositions other than P [11] (S in the above example), so that the upshot of the argument is to face the interlocutor with a forced choice between the original proposition, P, and the premise(s) from which the contradictory of P was deduced. In the above example the forced choice is, 'not-P or not-S': both P and S can't be true. If more than one premise had been used to derive not-P, say three, S, U, V, the upshot would be more complex, 'not-P or not-S or not-U or not-V—at least one of these four propositions must be false; all four can't be true at once.

Now, clearly, to practice a method and to understand exactly what one is doing in the course of it are two quite different things. That Socrates had some understanding of his own method goes without saying; but how complete was it? When he stopped to reflect on what he was doing he would lack an extremely useful tool of analysis: that of using letters to stand for propositions, as I have been doing here. Without some such technique it is very hard to see at a glance the form of the argu-

[11] On this point R. Robinson's fine analysis of the Socratic elenchus needs correction. He says that Plato "habitually *wrote as if* the falsehood followed from the refutant without the aid of an extra premise," *Plato's Earlier Dialectic,* Oxford, 1953, p. 28. For criticisms of this view see the reviews of the first edition of Robinson's book by P. Friedländer, *Classical Philology* 40 (1945), p. 253, and H. Cherniss, *American Journal of Philology,* 68 (1947), p. 136.

ment, and thus to get the point which is so obvious in the above description, namely, that the conclusion of a Socratic argument could never amount to the proof that the refutant, P, is false, *unless,* its contradictory, not-P, were deduced from no other premise than P itself, and that since this practically never happens,[12] the only result one can hope for is the demonstration of the incompatibility of P with the other propositions that figured as premises in the argument. This last would, of course, fall a long way short of proving that P is false. Thus, if our additional premises were $S, U, V,$ the upshot would not be, 'We can now be certain that P is false,' but only, 'We would be certain that P is false if we were certain that S and U and V were true.'

Was Socrates alive to this? If he had been perfectly clear about it in his own mind, he would have talked rather differently from the way he does. He would have regularly put his conclusions in the form of a disjunction ('not-P or not-S or . . .');[13] and this is hardly what he does. Thus he concludes his first argument in the Second Round with "According to this argument also wisdom would be courage,"[14] instead of 'According to this argument *either* wisdom is courage *or* at least one of our other premises is false.' In the case of the second argument in the First Round he comes closer to the required pattern, casting the conclusion in the form of a disjunction:[15]

> . . . which of the two assertions shall we renounce? One says that everything has but one opposite; the other that wisdom is distinct from self-control (*sophrosynē*) and . . . dissimilar (with it). . . . Which of these two assertions shall we renounce?[16]

[12] Except perhaps at *Euthyd.* 286c.

[13] I am not suggesting that he would have stuck mechanically to this pattern; logical pedantry is excluded by the spontaneity of a live discussion. But if he were quite clear about the essential point, he would have got it across in spite of ellipses and other variations.

[14] 350c. The logic of this argument will be scrutinized in the following section.

[15] To be more precise, an exclusive disjunction of the negates of the two propositions, 'not-P or not-V but not (both not-P and not-V).'

[16] 333a.

But unfortunately he makes the mistake of reducing the disjunction to *two* propositions, while it should consist of (at least) four, since not-*P* ('Wisdom is not different from *Sophrosynē*') has been deduced from

S. Wisdom and Folly are Opposites.

U. *Sophrosynē* and Folly are Opposites.

V. Everything (which has an opposite) has only one opposite.[17]

Thus the conclusion should have been, 'Which of the *four* assertions shall we renounce?' and the forced choice should not have been between *P* and *V*, where *V* is the undeniably true proposition (true by definition), 'Everything (which has an opposite) has only one opposite,' [18] but between four propositions, one of which is the miserably lame duck, *U*,[19] '*Sophrosynē* and Folly are opposites'—a far weaker proposition than *P*.

[17] 332a–e. To simplify matters I do not include any of the propositions which were merely used for the deduction of any of the above premises.

[18] The fact that Socrates goes through the motions of establishing it brings out beautifully how far short of true induction Socratic *epagogē* may fall; all that happens here is a reference to some instances which *exhibit the meaning of the statement* by exemplifying it, rather than *prove* it; it is really only what logicians call "intuitive induction," and this, as has been pointed out (M. R. Cohen and E. Nagel, *Introduction to Logic and Scientific Method*, New York, 1934, p. 275), "cannot be called an *inference*. . . . It is not a type of argument analyzable into a premise and a conclusion. It is a perception of relations . . . ."

[19] Deduced by the shadiest of logic. The crucial inference is at 332b from 'Acting foolishly implies acting without *sophrosynē*' to 'Acting foolishly is the opposite of acting with *sophrosynē*.' The fallacy will be obvious if one compares 'Being triangular implies being not square; therefore, being a triangular figure is the opposite of being a square figure,' noting that by the same reasoning one can 'prove' that a triangular figure is the opposite of a round one, whence, in conjunction with *V* above, one may infer, 'a square figure is not different from a round one.' Some of the commentators do strange things with this fallacy, particularly A. E. Taylor, who (*op. cit.*, 249) refuses to see here anything but the verbal idiom which facilitates it ("the fact that profligacy happens to be spoken of in Greek as 'folly,' ") and even this he excuses by finding in it "valuable evidence of the truth of the main tenet of Socratic morality." P. Shorey, *What Plato Said*, Chicago, 1933, p. 126, thinks there is a deliberate fallacy, but adduces evidence which, instead of proving his point, only confirms the suspicion that he is far from

But in spite of this kind of fuzziness as to the exact results obtained by particular arguments, Socrates seems perfectly clear about the (far more important) fact that his method neither assumes nor affords certainty about the truth or falsehood of any one proposition,[20] and that its purpose is a more modest one: to increase one's insight into the logical relations between propositions and thus one's ability to estimate how the truth claims of one proposition are affected by those of others, implying it or implied by it. Socrates seems to be telling us something like this all along: 'I am not undertaking to show you that this which I believe is true, and that which you maintain is false. All I am going to do is to investigate with you how either of them is related to a number of other things, so that you can see for yourself what commitments you are making *if* you accept the truth of your premise. Whatever decision you take will have to be yours.' And at this point he would have added almost certainly, 'I can't make it for you, because I don't *know*, I only *inquire*.' His profession of agnosticism, so puzzling when taken out of context, makes good sense when seen as part of his own method. He himself makes this junction and thereby gives us good evidence that he is fully aware of the point I am here suggesting:

> Critias, you act as though I professed to know the answers to the questions I ask you, and could give them to you, if I wished. It isn't so. I inquire with you into whatever is proposed just because I don't myself have knowledge.[21]

Had Socrates thought of his method as aiming at a certain demonstration of particular truths, he would not have talked this

---

clear as to just what the fallacy is. Friedländer, *Platon*, II, Leipzig, 1930, p. 17, understands the fallacy well enough, but he, too, thinks it intentional, and on grounds which I find no better than Shorey's.

[20] I.e., the material truth or falsehood of propositions of the order of *P, Q*, etc. He does seem certain about (at least some) hypotheticals of the order of '*P* implies *Q*.'

[21] *Charm.* 165b; cf. *Gorg.* 506a. There is no fully comparable statement in the *Protagoras*, but the point of view is implicit (a) in his brief description at 348c of his reason for getting into these arguments (note 9 above), and (b) its reiteration at 360e and 361d, along with (c) his final admission of puzzlement at 361c.

way unless he were conceding that his previous practice of his method had been a failure, and this he would not have admitted for a moment. On the contrary, we find him reiterating his profession of agnosticism at a moment when he feels it has been completely successful:

> These things became so evident in our previous arguments that they are held fast and bound, if I may speak so bluntly, by arguments of iron and adamant. . . . But as for me, my position is always the same: I have no knowledge whether these things are true or not.[22]

The man who says, 'Not-P is the conclusion of an argument that is as strong as it could be. But is not-P true? I don't know,' has grasped the essential feature of his method. He has seen that its aim cannot be final demonstrative certainty, and that its practice is quite compatible with suspended judgment as to the material truth of any one of its conclusions.

3. How Good is His Logic?

Almost everything Socrates says is wiry argument; that is the beauty of his talk for a philosopher. So we can't dodge the question whether or not the wires are joined together by valid inferences, though neither could we answer it fully without getting into technicalities for which there is no room in this brief Introduction. As a reasonable compromise, I offer an analysis of the main points in the first argument of the Second Round.[23] I choose this one because its logic was loudly protested by Protagoras,[24] and the rights and wrongs of this dispute have never been properly cleared up in the literature. Here it is, stripped down to its formal propositions: [25]

22 *Gorg.* 508e–509a.
23 349d–350c.
24 350c–351b.
25 Slightly rephrased to make their logical form more perspicuous. I must preface this analysis by making it clear that my knowledge of logic is elementary. This should encourage readers who know little or no modern logic, and put on their guard those who know a great deal.

A. All the Brave are Confident.

B. All Virtue is Noble.

Ba. All the Brave are Noble.

C. All the Wise are Confident.

D. Some Confident men are not Wise.

E. No Confident men who are not Wise are Noble.

Therefore (in consequence of *E* and *Ba* above),[26]

F. No Confident men who are not Wise are Brave.

But also,

G. All Wise men who are Confident are Brave.

Therefore (in consequence of *C* and *G*),[27]

H. All the Wise are Brave.

Let us go down these propositions and check Socrates' warrant for asserting each one: *A* is admitted without argument.[28] So is *B*.[29] *Ba* is not spelled out in the text, no doubt because it follows so obviously from *B*.[30] *C* is supported by reasoning that will be looked into in the following section; for the present we

---

[26] The argument falls into the form of a *Camestres* syllogism if we take 'Confident men who are not Wise' as a single term.

[27] A perfectly valid argument, which cannot be put into Aristotelian form, but can be easily handled by the class calculus:

$$C. \; w\bar{c} = O$$
$$G. \; wc\bar{b} = O; \text{ hence, by the elimination of } \bar{c} \text{ and } c,$$
$$H. \; w\bar{b} = O$$

[28] 349e. Indeed overadmitted, according to the present translation, "When you speak of brave men, do you mean the confident . . . " But since (a) it is also possible to translate, "Do you say that the brave are confident . . ." (so e.g. Croiset-Bodin, Apelt), and (b) Protagoras later repudiates the equivalence of "brave" and "confident," it is best to settle for the minimum concession at this point, as I have done at *A*. Even *A*, it should be added, would not express Socrates' own thought without qualification, since his later definition of courage (360d) implies that there are things which the brave man can and does fear. To do justice to this one would have to expand *A* into 'All the brave are confident in respect of those things which they ought not to fear,' a complication which can be ignored in this context.

[29] *Loc. cit.*

[30] In conjunction with (the evidently true) 'Courage is a Virtue,' *B* implies 'Courage is Noble,' which I have put into extensional form in *Ba* to make it homogeneous with *E* for the deduction of *F*.

need only notice that it satisfies Protagoras, and that he freely admits C.[31] D is agreed to right off.[32] And Protagoras very cooperatively supplies the remark which establishes E.[33] Then taking E with Ba above, F certainly follows. So far Socrates has behaved according to the rules. He has used no proposition except those admitted by Protagoras. One may complain that Protagoras has been made to agree too easily. But that is another story and does not invalidate in the least the contention that Socrates has not been guilty of any logical foul.

But what of G? Has Socrates established this? No. Has he got Protagoras' consent to it? No. *Could* he have got it by deducing it formally from the admitted statements? Again, no. Clearly then he has no business to assert it, as he undeniably does at 350c.[34] Protagoras then has good reason for making a complaint—but not for the complaint he makes. He says Socrates imputes to him the admission of the converse of A,

I. All the Confident are Brave,

and has used I to prove his case. Now certainly I *could* have been used to derive the conclusion Socrates is fishing for,[35] but Socrates would have been an utter fool to use it for this or any other purpose. Far from having any interest in getting Protag-

31 350a.

32 350b.

33 *Loc. cit.* Fully spelled out,

> *Da.* All Confident men who are not Wise are Mad.
>
> *Db.* No Mad men are Noble.

Therefore,

> *E.* No Confident men who are not Wise are Noble.

34 Very hastily and not as lucidly as he should have: ". . . and (*sc.* the wise) being most confident are also bravest," which *could* be taken to mean 'the wise are bravest, because all who are most confident are bravest,' instead of 'the wise who are most confident are bravest.' The ambiguity of meaning in the grammatical form is the immediate source of Protagoras' error: he reads it in the first way; why it must be read in the second will be explained directly.

35   *I.* All the Confident are Brave.

> *C.* All the Wise are Confident.

Therefore,

> *H.* All the Wise are Brave.

oras to admit I, Socrates has the strongest interest to show him that I is false. Socrates' whole concept of courage requires him to mark it off in the sharpest terms from something else ("confidence") which is popularly confused with courage, and this, of course, is the reason why he has taken the time to prove F. He could hardly wish to surrender this major objective,[36] which is what he would have to do *if* he had assumed the truth of I.[37] So while Socrates has made a mistake, Protagoras mistakes the nature of this mistake.

Is the result then a stalemate? Far from it. In the immediate argument Socrates' position is incomparably stronger—not because he can prove G from premises admitted by Protagoras, but because he does not need to prove it to win the immediate argument, and he already holds in his own hand all the cards he needs for just this purpose. For what *is* he trying to do at the moment? To disprove the last statement made by Protagoras (349d), the relevant part of which boils down to the assertion that some people, while very brave, are most ignorant (i.e. not wise). To disprove this, Socrates must prove its contradictory,

J. All the Brave are Wise,

[36] I put less weight on the formal inconsistency (F in conjunction with D implies the contradictory of I), since this (it might be argued) Socrates overlooked through a possible logical slip.

[37] That is why the verbal ambiguity in his statement must be resolved in the second of the two ways mentioned in note 34, above. Another reason is to maintain the symmetry with the previous proposition, F (which was asserted immediately before, at 350c 1-2): the natural complement to 'All Confident men who are *not* Wise are *not* Brave' is 'All Confident men who *are* Wise *are* Brave' (which is the equivalent of G), hardly 'All Confident men are Brave.' The reader may feel I am laboring the obvious. But if he will consult other good translations (e.g. Apelt's, or the Croiset-Bodin), he will see that their translation favors the *first* of the two readings, in which case one would have to concede Protagoras' objection (so e.g. H. Räder, *Platons Philosophische Entwicklung*, Leipzig, 1905, pp. 109-110); it will not do to ignore the logical force of the objection (as unfortunately many good commentators do) or openly dismiss it as trivial (so Shorey, *op. cit.*, p. 129), for if Socrates has made the mistake alleged by Protagoras, he has blundered hopelessly. Of all the commentators I have consulted on this point Nestle alone (*ad loc.*, in his commentary) has the correct interpretation.

not H, 'All the Wise are Brave';[38] and since he need not prove *H* for the purpose in hand, neither does he need *G,* whose only use to him in the argument would have been that of a stepping-stone to *H.* And *J* he can easily prove from premises already admitted by Protagoras:

A. All the Brave are Confident.
F. No Confident men who are not Wise are Brave.
Therefore,
J. All the Brave are Wise.[39]

Yet neither can we resolve the dispute entirely in Socrates' favor. For though, as I have said, *J* is all he needs to prove just now, he can't afford to drop *H* permanently. What he is arguing for is that the concepts of courage and wisdom are coextensive; and to do this he must show not only *J,* 'All the brave are wise,' but also *H,* 'All the wise are brave.' How he will do this (if he can) is his own affair. All we need point out is that his ill-starred effort to prove *H* did not result from a mere logical blunder. He was right in thinking that he had to prove it, though wrong in the way he thought he proved it.

I trust I have made it clear that Socrates' performance in this argument is much better than would appear from the fact, which it would be folly to hush up, that he has made a definite error.[40] For the error he does make is one that he could easily have detected when he got the chance to think out his moves in a more leisurely moment. He would then have seen that he *could* have produced a valid deductive argument for his immediate objective, and did not have to revoke a single inference he had made. And although some Socratic arguments are worse

38 Whose truth is obviously compatible with that of 'Some who are not Wise are Brave.'

39 Another perfectly valid inference which cannot be turned into an Aristotelian syllogism, but can easily be validated algebraically as at note 27, above.

40 —not a formal fallacy, since no mistake was made in any of the formal inferences; all three of them (notes 26, 27, 33) are perfectly valid, though each of them involves one premise with *three* terms, and is thus distinctly more complicated than an ordinary Aristotelian syllogism.

than this one,[41] most of them are a good deal better. Many are formally valid; and most of those which are not could probably have been made so by Socrates himself by a different use of his premises or by the use of different premises of much the same order of plausibility. This is not to deny that he occasionally makes grave errors; we shall see one of them in the following section. It is only to insist that as a practitioner of logical inference, and one who practices on his feet, in the stress of live debate, and with no calculus or any formal patterns of valid inference to guide him, Socrates is not a bungler, but a master. Whatever inadequacies infect his serious philosophical doctrines, though they often involve logical slips, are not *due* to such slips, but to another weakness which we must now consider.

4. The Weakness of His Method

Let us look more closely at one of the propositions in the preceding argument: *C*. 'All the Wise are Confident.' The "confident" Socrates is talking about are men with 'spunk' or 'nerve,' "those who are ready to go at things which others are afraid to approach." [42] What he wants us to believe is that all who have "knowledge" or "wisdom" will have such immunity to fear. And why so? Because three classes of people who have "knowledge"—skilled divers, cavalry-men, peltasts [43]—are more "con-

[41] See note 19, above; and section (5), below, *sub fin.* For the odd error at 330cd see "The Third Man Argument in the *Parmenides*," *Philosophical Review* 63 (1954), pp. 337–38; G. Grote, *Plato*, II, London, 1865, p. 51; O. Apelt, *Platons Dialog Protagoras*, Leipzig, 1918, note *ad loc.*; A. Koyré, *Discovering Plato*, New York, 1945, pp. 26–28.

[42] 349e. Another good clue to its meaning is that the Greek *tharros* is used as the opposite of "fear" (360b, *Laws* 644c; Arist. *Rhet.* 1383a 16), and is thought of as a "passion," i.e., an emotional state (*Tim.* 69d; Arist. *de Anima* 403a 7–17) in a much more direct sense than is conveyed by the English "confidence" ("mental attitude of trusting in or relying on" given as the primary sense in the *Shorter Oxford English Dictionary*, whose primary sense for "fear" begins "the emotion of . . .").

[43] Light-armed troops, at this time generally mercenaries, in contrast

fident" than those who don't have it, and each of their members is more "confident" after acquiring this "knowledge" than he was before. "And that is true of all other cases," [44] Protagoras obligingly volunteers, and the argument is complete. Now we are supposed to have been shown that if only a man has "knowledge," he will face without fear any danger he chooses to face; alarms which panic others will not touch him. One looks at this and rubs one's eyes in amazement at the thought that such fragile threads of evidence are expected to support such an enormous conclusion. What sort of reasoning does Socrates think he is making? He seems to be offering us an induction: [45] X is true in cases $a, b, c,$ of the class Y; therefore, X must be true in all cases of Y. The premise is presumably a matter of observation; has Socrates then done some empirical research into the psychology of divers, cavalry-men, peltasts, and is he reporting its results? Moreover, if the conclusion were to follow, all cases of Y would have to be homogeneous with the odd samples in the premise. Has Socrates established this? Has he shown that, when we talk of my "knowledge" that it is wrong to harm my enemy and the peltasts' "knowledge" of the right way to use a shield, we are talking about the same thing and may thus extrapolate statements about the former from statements about the latter? Socrates does not seem to realize that such questions affect the substance of his reasoning, else he would not have ignored them. The reason he disappoints us is that his *method* does not recognize the importance of such queries. In working out the logical relations of given premises to one another he is as careful as one can expect him to be, considering that formal logic is still in its prenatal stage; he moves a step at a time, insuring, to the best of his ability, that each step will be a sound,

---

to the heavy-armed citizen soldier, or hoplite, to be mentioned below, Section (5).

44 350a.

45 A *bona fide* one (i.e., probable inference from sample) it would have to be this time, in contrast to the 'intuitive induction' at 332c (note 18, above). I know of not a single word in the Socratic dialogues to suggest that Socrates was aware of the vast difference between these two superficially similar uses of *epagogē*. Cf. Robinson, *op. cit.*, p. 36.

logical inference. But when it comes to assessing the support which this or that premise can get from observed or observable facts, Socrates seems quite satisfied with acrobatic jumps to reckless conclusions from remote, shaky, and dubiously relevant data.

Far more important than *C* for Socrates is the proposition he announces so dramatically, if not melodramatically, at 352a-c, and to whose proof he devotes the best part of the ensuing argument, the most massive in the whole argument.[46] The traditional formula for it is:

> *K*. Knowledge is Virtue,[47]

and we may use it for the Socratic doctrine that anyone who knows what is the best course of action open to him in any given situation cannot fail to follow it. Socrates' later statement for it is worth quoting, if only because its ponderous and repetitious formulation, so rare for him, underlines in still another way the vast importance he attaches to it:

> No man voluntarily pursues evil, or that which he thinks to be evil. To pursue what one believes to be evil rather than what is good *is not in human nature*; and when a man is compelled to choose one of two evils, no one will choose the greater when he may have the less.[48]

46 351b–358d is Socrates' counterweight, in length and substance, to Protagoras' Great Speech, and, as I remarked above, it reaches its climax at 356de in the refutation of "the power of appearance." It is as though Socrates were willing to pit this one argument, all by itself, against the tacit premise of Protagoras' Great Speech, moral subjectivism, confident that this alone would carry the day.

47 Though usually given in the form of 'Virtue is Knowledge,' without distinguishing the two formulae required to express the two quite different things asserted by Socrates: that knowledge is (i) the necessary and (ii) the sufficient condition of virtuous action. It is better to keep 'Virtue is Knowledge' for (i), except where 'is' stands for '='.

48 358cd, where it is presented as that which has been *proved* by the argument which starts at 351b. In the earlier formulation of the demonstrant (352bd) Socrates is, by contrast, even more spontaneous and informal than is his wont; he starts very solemnly, but quite imprecisely, at 352b, and it is only when he gets to 352d 4–e 2 that one sees exactly what he is driving at.

The words which are italicized show quite well what kind of statement Socrates is making here: the kind which we would call an empirical one. *K*, like its humbler cousin, *C*, purports to tell us a fact of human nature—the kind of matter of fact that can only be found out by observation. Where then is the reference to such observation? Nowhere in the whole of this elaborate argument. In the case of *C* Socrates at least went through the motions of induction; here not even this: he is quite content here with a purely *deductive* proof of it. Now anyone who could excogitate by pure deduction a fact of human nature would have to be more than a master of argument—he would have to be a wizard. And as Socrates is only human, we would not be risking much if we were to predict that his attempt will fail. Let us look at his argument. Here is a simplified version of the essential points:

'Grant that (*L*) the pleasant and the good are identical, and it will then be shown that no one who knows the good will fail to do it, if he can. For what could prevent him from doing it? The only plausible answer would be *pleasure*.[48a] But if *good* and *pleasant* are equivalent terms, to know that *x* is best is to know that *x* is most pleasant (either immediately or in its eventual consequences). But *it is* surely *absurd to say that (M) pleasure could prevent one from doing the most pleasant thing*.[49] Therefore, one will always do the good if one knows it and can do it (= *K*).'

48a I am glossing over here an odd hiatus in the argument. While at 352b anger, love, fear are included among the things that the "many" think can overpower knowledge, and this is recalled at 352e, suddenly, at 352e-353a the passions drop out and Socrates starts talking as though pleasure (and pain) were the only opponents of reason worth talking about.

49 355a, "If what you say is true [i.e., if *L* is true], then the statement is absurd which affirms that a man often does evil knowingly, when he might abstain, because he is seduced or overpowered by pleasure . . ." Then Socrates proceeds to ring the changes on the "absurdities" which are involved here. The reader should be warned that the Greek word here translated by "absurd," *geloion*, means only "ridiculous," but the tenor of Socrates' argument makes it quite clear that he does think logical absurdity is involved.

I have lettered the initial identification of the pleasant with the good, but not because I think it the soft spot of the argument. It is certainly puzzling that Socrates should hang the whole proof of his great proposition, *K*, from what looks to us like a declaration of hedonism.[50] For hedonism is not in keep-

[50] It has been generally so taken and (mainly on this ground) the majority of the commentators have held that *L* is not Socrates' own opinion, but "the unconscious Hedonism of the average man" (Taylor, *op. cit.*, 260; cf. F. M. Cornford, *Cambridge Ancient History*, VI p. 313) or, more subtly, a reduction of "the qualified hedonism of the masses and (by implication at least) of Protagoras" to "hedonism pure" (G. Grube, *Plato's Thought*, London, 1935, p. 60, and cf. his article in *Classical Quarterly* 27 (1933), pp. 203ff.; further variations in J. Moreau, *Construction de l'Idéalisme Platonicien*, Paris, 1939, pp. 62ff., and others). For the minority view which I believe much more nearly right, see especially R. Hackforth, "Hedonism in Plato's *Protagoras*," *Classical Quarterly* 22 (1928), pp. 39ff.; also G. Grote, *op. cit.*, pp. 87–89. My main reason for rejecting the majority view is that it is most unlikely that Socrates would deliberately offer a false proposition as a premise for establishing his great proposition, *K*: where one proposition implies another, the falsehood of the first does not, of course, impugn the truth of the second, but neither does it do anything to establish it; and in this context to make *L* the premise for *K* would have been extremely misleading, for it would have encouraged the listener to *believe a falsehood*, and this Socrates, being what he is, would never do unless he put in clear and sufficient warning signs, of which *there is not one* in this argument: the repeated question to the "many," whether they can propose any standard other than pleasure (354be) is nothing of the kind, for it doesn't in the least imply that there *is* some such other standard. Contrast the case of the *Hippias Minor*, where Socrates makes perfectly plain his reservations about the proposition which he defends in argument but does not accept without qualification (that 'if one errs deliberately, he is a better man than one who errs involuntarily') by (a) voicing uncertainty at 372de (and again at 376c) as to the truth of the hypothetical, (b) leaving open the question of the truth of the antecedent by adding pointedly at 376b, "if there be such a man" (sc. who errs voluntarily). Neither (a) nor (b) have any counterpart for *L* in the *Protagoras*, where they would be needed far more urgently, since the obviously paradoxical nature of the proposition in the *Hp. Min.* is itself a sufficient warning, while there is nothing obviously paradoxical about *L*. Contrast *L* also with 'Virtue cannot be Taught,' over which Socrates wavers at 319ab, 320b, is openly perplexed at 361ac. (Cf. also Conclusion, note 13.)

ing with the general temper or method of Socratic ethics: Socrates *never* seeks to answer the question 'Is *x* the morally best thing?' by inquiring whether or not *x* is the most pleasant thing to do and, having satisfied himself that it is, arguing that it is *therefore* morally best.[51] But the puzzle is not insoluble. What Socrates most likely meant to assert is the rather different proposition, or rather two of them, (a) that pleasure is *a* good (not the only one), (b) that whatever is best will *in fact* be the most pleasant. (a) and (b) do not add up to hedonism, i.e. to making pleasure *definitive* of good; there is nothing to keep a man from asserting, as Plato did in his mature philosophy (and so did Aristotle), both (a) and (b), without *defining* the good in terms of the pleasant.[52] But though this is true, it is by no means obvious at first sight, and it would be perfectly possible for Socrates to have failed to understand a matter which no one had as yet explained or even properly investigated, and thus assert *L* when all he in fact *intended* to assert was (a) and (b). But even if he *had* intended *L*, there would be nothing formally wrong with its assertion in this argument. It would be odd that

51 Thus, in this dialogue, in the case of his new concept of courage (to be discussed in the next section) Socrates does not argue 'this kind of courage is pleasantest, therefore it is best,' but, in effect, 'this is the only kind of courage that is *noble*,' where "noble," *kalon*, is his nearest equivalent for our 'morally good.' In no case does he argue '*x* is noble because it is pleasant,' but he may (and does at 359e and 360a) '*x* is pleasant because it is noble.'

52 Plato accepts (a) in the *Philebus* by arguing for the superiority of the "Mixed Life" (pleasure and intelligence); he argues for (b) at length in the *Republic* (Book IX), a position he could not afford to abandon later on, for he maintained to the end of his life (*Laws* 660e ff., 732e ff.) that no man will ever choose the less pleasant of any two courses of action open to him. Plato nevertheless refused (e.g. at *Phil.* 60a) to *identify* the pleasant and the good. Nevertheless, beginning with the *Gorgias* (495a ff.), Plato consistently rejects *L*; at *Phil.* 60 he denies *L*, formulating it in the same terms in which Socrates affirms it at *Prot.* 355b. An easy way to solve our puzzle would be to read back to the *Protagoras* Plato's later views, weakening *L* to (b): so M. Pohlenz, *Aus Platos Werdezeit*, Berlin, 1913, p. 106; his evidence is 358b! For Aristotle's view see W. D. Ross, *Aristotle*, London, 1949, (5th edition), pp. 225ff.

Socrates would want to do this: that is the worst we could have then said; we could not have convicted him here of positive error because of this.

And that is precisely what we can do in the case of that very plausible statement which I have underlined. *M* is *not* absurd, though it certainly looks as if it were. To see that it is not, compare *N* and *O*:

> *N.* I ought to do what is most pleasant; *x* is most pleasant; I ought not to do *x*.
>
> *O.* I ought to do what is most pleasant; *x* is most pleasant; I shall not do *x*.

That there *is* absurdity in *N* is obvious. Its first two statements imply 'I ought to do *x*'; hence to assert *N* is to assert the contradiction, 'I ought to do *x* and I ought not to do *x*.' No such contradiction occurs at *O*, for in 'I ought to do *x*, but I shall not do it,' both statements may be true (as, e.g., in 'I ought to stop smoking, but I shan't'). Now *M* would be as absurd as Socrates says it is, if, like *N*, it asserted or implied (in conjunction with the initial assumption that the pleasant is the good and hence, for Socrates, that which I ought to do) that I ought not to do the most pleasant thing open to me, and then proceeded to compound the absurdity by saying that I ought not to do it on account of pleasure! But that is not at all what *M* means in its own context (what it has to mean to do the job that is required of it in this argument)[53]: it refers to cases, like those envisaged at *O* (*not N*), in which I don't do that which it is assumed I ought to do, namely, the thing which will yield the

[53] I add this because in the sequel, 355d, Socrates starts talking as though the absurdity in being "overcome by pleasure" is the implication that pleasure was "not worthy" to overcome (i.e. did not deserve to do so, or, ought not to do so); for one who had already agreed to *L*, this would certainly *be* absurd. But the statement at 355a (the original for my "it is absurd to say *M*") is that it is absurd to say that a man *can* be (*not*, 'deserves to be') overcome by pleasure. The confusion in Socrates' mind is evident in this shift from 'can' to 'is worthy of' (for the sense in which Plato uses the term, *axios*, translated as "worthy" here, cf. 358c, where it is clearly a value term, and is translated as "important").

greatest pleasure; and it adds: and pleasure is what (causally) prevents me from doing it. Is there anything absurd about this? May not the pull of an immediate pleasure "seduce" me and make me spurn the course of action that would produce the greatest long-run pleasure?[53a] Or, to think of the corresponding situation in terms of pain: a sharp present pain may, and often enough does, cause the avoidance of a course of action (say, a cautery where anesthetics are unavailable) which would be less painful by far in the long run. M, therefore, does not involve absurdity; and to say that it does is to confuse it with a proposition related to M as N is to O.[54]

The most interesting thing here is not *that* Socrates makes this mistake, but the reason *why* he makes it. He would have been far less likely to make it had he clearly understood what is implied in his own words—namely that K, if true, is true as a fact of "human nature"; and, like C above, asserts the conjunction of two logically distinct things, an intellectual state (knowing or believing something), and an emotional one (one in which there is the affective backing for doing the thing one knows or believes one ought to do); and that, again like C, to assert this kind of conjunction involves an *estimate of the facts*, so that the whole issue boils down to the question whether Socrates' estimate of the facts is right or not. Euripides in his

[53a] A common defense for Socrates is to (i) concede "seduction" by pleasure but contend that (ii) at the moment it occurs one *no longer* knows or believes one is doing wrong (so e.g. A. E. Taylor, *Socrates*, London, 1951, p. 150). This gets closer to the facts, admitting 'rationalization' at (i), but not close enough, since (ii) is not always true. Anyhow, Socrates could not afford this defense for it would trivialize his K, conceding to passion to "master" knowledge after all.

[54] The reader should be warned that some current writing on moral theory veers round to something approaching the statement of Socrates which I have been criticizing, though for reasons quite different from his. Thus P. H. Nowell-Smith, *Ethics*, London, 1954, p. 178: "It is logically odd to say 'This is the (morally) better course; but I shall do that' (cf. pp. 260ff.)." "Odd" here does not, of course, refer to outright contradiction, but to some more subtle (and obscure) incongruity. I maintain that "It would be (morally) better for me to stop smoking, but I shall not' is no more "logically odd" than it is logically absurd; it is just morally pitiful.

Medea (produced in 432, so shortly after the dramatic date of our dialogue), addressing himself to just this question,[55] declared flatly for the negative. In a monologue which is the 'center of gravity' of the play [56] Medea deliberates whether or not she will murder her children, and when she makes the fatal decision, she declares:

> I know what evil I am about to do. But passion is stronger than my resolutions—passion, the cause of men's worst acts.[57]

The man she has loved has drawn away from her. Her only way to touch him now is "to stab his heart."[58] Her love for him, now turned to hate, forces her hand in action, leaving her intellect completely lucid, yet utterly powerless to prevent what she well knows will bring her "double the harm"[59] it will cause him. "You will become the most miserable of women," implores the Chorus. She replies: "So be it. Vain are all moderate words."[60] So here on the stage before our eyes Euripides gives Socrates the lie. Who is right? The trouble with Socrates is not so much that he was wrong on this point (and I, for one, unquestionably think he was) as that his method did not provide him with the means by which he would be likely to correct or, at least, suspect his own error. He was too fascinated by the patterns into which he could organize his propositions to reflect with the needed sensitiveness and humility on matters which can only be learned from the facts themselves or from those whose vision of the facts is more subtle and penetrating than one's own. Had his method been less narrow he might have sensed how false

55 Cf. the recent remarks of B. Snell, "Das frühste Zeugnis über Sokrates," *Philologus* 97 (1948), pp. 125ff.; E. R. Dodds, *The Greeks and the Irrational,* Berkeley, 1951, p. 186, who also refers to earlier discussions at p. 199, n. 47.

56 B. Snell, *The Discovery of the Mind,* Engl. transl. by T. G. Rosenmeyer, Oxford, 1953, p. 124, remarks that the play "is wholly written around the monologue."

57 *Vv.* 1078–80.

58 *V.* 1360.

59 *V.* 1047, preceded at 1044, and followed at 1048, by "good-bye, my resolutions."

60 *Vv.* 818–19.

was his metaphor at the end of the mock-exegesis of Simonides, how much more than entertainment a moral philosopher could get from poets and others who are no great arguers but know the human heart.

5. The Great Teacher

Infallibility is not required for this role, else it would never have been filled. A man may be mistaken in a hundred ways, and still qualify if even one of the things he taught was important enough for his time. Socrates' method was such a thing. To criticize its misuse, as I have been doing, must not obscure the fact that some use of the deductive method is indispensable for almost every kind of mature philosophizing; only a pure romantic or a mystic would reject it on principle. Before Socrates it had already found its masters in Parmenides and Zeno. Socrates did more than import it to the new field of ethics which the sophists were opening up. He used it in a way whose novelty caught the fresh eye of his contemporaries. Protagoras picks it up right in the middle of our dialogue: "According to your favorite mode of speech, Socrates, 'let us investigate this,' he said . . ."[61]—and how? By exploring relations of implication and incompatibility between the proposed statement and all sorts of others, suspending judgment as to its truth or falsehood in the meantime. To pursue this method of "hypothesis"[62] in live debate, not merely from time to time, or as a mere preliminary to something else, but so persistently that to philosophize was to practice this kind of "investigating" and "examining,"[63] no more and no less, insisting all the while, 'I don't know, I

---

[61] 351e.

[62] The contrast between the Socratic (for examples see Robinson, *op. cit.*, p. 111; also *Prot.* 361b, *Gorg.* 454c) and earlier uses of this term in philosophy is dramatically illustrated by the fact that the Hippocratic treatises (see *Gnomon* 27 (1955), p. 68, n. 1) use it exclusively to refer to far-flung cosmological theories which, needless to say, were not presented as hypotheses in our sense of the term, but as speculative dogmas.

[63] Cf. *Ap.* 28e.

only inquire,' secure without certainty—this was as new as anything ever is under the sun. What was not new was the one-
sidedness with which he gave himself over to his innovation.
The greatness of Greek philosophy had been its intellectual
daring; its weakness, impatience with uncongenial truth. Socrates was in that tradition. In the extremism of his method he
was the kin of Heraclitus and Parmenides.

As instructive as the exhibition of the method itself were
some of the by-products of making it the method of philosophical conversation. Instead of having (as in a Protagorean Great
Speech) a great number of propositions thrown at you in quick
succession, uncertainties as to their meaning piling up in your
mind, so that you soon give up the effort to clear up any of
them and are content to catch the bare drift of the discourse,
in a Socratic discussion you can stop the speaker at any point
with a 'Just what do you mean by that?' and air each obscurity
the very moment it is felt. And the very fact that you are required to say whether or not you agree to each proposition as it
is put before you, one at a time, gives you a high incentive to
press for clarification, for you may soon look like a fool if you
agree to something without understanding what exactly you
agreed to. Under such conditions you become sensitized to the
importance of drawing exact boundaries between superficially
similar terms, starting, for the first time in Western philosophy,
the systematic quest for definitions.[64] You also come to see how
essential to clear thinking is Socrates' concentration on the
"small"[65] point, the fine distinction, the "scrapings and shav-
ings of an argument,"[66] as they look to the exasperated Hippias.

[64] A matter which is the main business of several Socratic dialogues,
e.g. the *Euthyphro*, the *Laches*, the *Charmides*, the *Hippias Major*. What we
get in this dialogue—a couple of definitions propounded by Socrates himself and at the very end of a discussion, to crystallize its results—is un-
representative. For Socratic Definition generally see Robinson, *op. cit.*,
Ch. V.

[65] A fine example at 329b. Cf. *Gorg.* 497bc, "Socrates is always like
that . . . , investigating and examining petty, insignificant things . . .
Go ahead, ask your finicky little questions . . ."

[66] *Hp. Maj.* 304a; cf. 301b.

Socrates' method makes you see how big in their consequences are matters that seem so picayune and piddling by themselves, and thus how worthy of serious inquiry are things which otherwise would have passed unnoticed.

If Socrates had done no more than this, his place as a philosophical teacher would have been secure. But we would still have to account for the man who made Alcibiades feel ashamed. Only a *moral* teacher could have done this, one who put men's lives, not just their opinions, on trial in philosophical arguments.[67] Socrates did this, and more. He made men feel that the life of all humanity was under judgment. "If you're serious, and what you say is true," says Callicles in the *Gorgias,* "won't human life have to be turned completely upside down?"[68] It is fashionable nowadays to hold that "it is not especially the business of the philosopher to make value judgments, to tell people how they ought to live."[69] Socrates made this very much his own business, and one of his contributions, I think his greatest, was that he did make value judgments, new ones and with far-reaching effects. Such was his reasoned denial of the age-old conviction that it is as right to harm one's enemies as it is to benefit one's friends.[70] In our dialogue we see another: his transformation of the idea of courage.

The two words which Socrates distinguishes so sharply, "confidence" (*tharros*) and "courage" (*andreia*), were interchanged freely in common speech. This looseness was deplorable for moral, not linguistic, reasons. It perpetuated a grossness

[67] 333c; cf. especially *Charm.* 188bc, *Ap.* 39cd.

[68] 481c; translation by W. C. Helmbold (in this series), also utilized in part in note 65, above.

[69] A. J. Ayer, describing the views of the "Vienna Circle," in *Revolution in Philosophy*, London, 1956, p. 78. For concurrence on this point by writers of different philosophical persuasions: F. H. Bradley, *Ethical Studies*, Second Edition, Oxford, 1927, pp. 199–200; G. E. Moore, *Principia Ethica*, Cambridge, 1903, p. 161; C. D. Broad, *Five Types of Ethical Theory*, London, 1930, Preface. (Socrates would make a perfect case of what Broad here calls amusingly "spiritual diabetes.")

[70] *Crito* 49bc; *Rep.* 335b–336a; cf. *Gorg.* 469b ff. The only Greek contemporary view which approaches the Socratic at this point is that of Democritus (Diels-Kranz, *op. cit.*, 68 B 45).

of perception, a failure to discriminate a nonmoral from a moral quality. The first can be displayed by animals as well as men; the other is that uniquely human achievement, the mastery of fear by a high sense of duty and a clear understanding of the reasons for which danger may have to be faced. Socrates' redefinition of courage as "the knowledge of what is and is not fearful"[71] is one way of marking out the difference. The effect is not just to correct obtuse appraisals of the moral worth of certain actions, but also to make new, more stringent, moral demands. Men who are endowed, by temperament or habituation, with a high threshold for fear may now be informed that the sheer ability to dash or plod through danger does not qualify them for the approval expressed by "brave"; something more is required of them—an understanding of the comparative moral worth of objects for which risks ought or ought not to be taken. Men of the other type, more sensitive, more imaginative, more vulnerable to emotional stress, not inured to danger in their previous mode of living, are reminded that the high imperative of courage rests on them too, and that they too have resources for meeting it, though at greater cost to themselves. When we have admitted to the full the limitations of the Socratic definition—its overestimation of the intellectual factor coupled with (and facilitated by) a failure to make clear what sort of "knowledge" is involved, how unlike that of the aforesaid divers, cavalrymen, peltasts—we may still accept it as the discovery of a new kind of courage, so different from the "confidence" with which the old could be, and was, confused, that it not only excludes "base confidence," but also includes "noble fear."[72]

A sober claim to novelty can afford to weigh just counterclaims. Here we must think of those of another person in our

[71] 360d; *Lach.* 194e.

[72] Implied by the definition, and at 360b.—What I have said about 'courage = knowledge' will apply *mutatis mutandis* to 'virtue = knowledge,' whose most valuable import would be likewise that of a redefinition of virtue and therewith the discovery of a new kind of virtue.

dialogue, the sophist Prodicus,[73] who gave much thought to linguistic distinctions.[74] There is good reason to suppose that one of those he worked out was that between "courage" and two related terms, "daring" (*tolmē*) and "boldness" (*thrasytēs*), with "foresight" (*promēthia*) as the differentiating property of courage.[75] The distinction was influential: Euripides[76] and Thucydides[77] took it up. Socrates, who knew Prodicus intimately,[78] would have been one of the first to hear it. How far

[73] For a good, brief account of his teachings, see K. Freeman, *Companion to the Pre-Socratic Philosophers*, Oxford, 1946, pp. 370–74; for fuller ones, H. Gomperz, *Sophistik und Rhetorik*, Leipzig, 1912, pp. 90ff., W. Nestle, *op. cit.*, pp. 349ff.

[74] Choice samples in our dialogue: 337a–c; 341ab; 358a.

[75] In the *Laches*, when Nicias distinguishes "boldness" and "daring" from "courage" on the basis of "foresight" (197b), Socrates remarks that he "has taken over this wisdom from our companion Damon, while Damon is a close associate of Prodicus, who is considered the best of all the sophists in making such verbal distinctions" (197d). The most natural reading of this passage is that Damon (on whom see K. Freeman, *op. cit.*, pp. 207–08) here is only the middleman, and that Socrates alludes to him merely because Nicias is Damon's friend. That Damon himself should be the author of this important distinction is possible, but less likely, since this kind of work was not his *métier*. Another possibility is that the ascription to Prodicus is ironical, Socrates himself being its real author; but the fact that "foresight" is the basis of the distinction here (and see next two notes) is quite enough to mark it off as un-Socratic: the last part of the *Laches* is a critique of the notion that courage consists of the knowledge of *future* good and evil.

[76] *Suppl.* 508–10: The herald cautions against the "bold" (*thrasys*) leader, and adds sententiously: "Let this be courage for you: foresight."

[77] 3.82.4, "Unreasoning *daring* was thought comradely *courage*, and *foresighted* concern for the future a pretense for *cowardice*." Cf. 2.40.3; 2.62.5. Cf. Marc., *Vita Thuc.* 36, a testimony to the influence of Prodicus on the style of Thucydides.

[78] He says he is Prodicus' "pupil," 341a, his 'educator,' *Meno* 96d (significant, in spite of the irony: Socrates does not speak of any other contemporary as his teacher, to my knowledge, with the trivial exception of Connus, who taught him the lyre, *Euthyd.* 272c, *Menex.* 235e). Prodicus is his "companion" (*Hp. Maj.* 282c); he has heard Prodicus making linguistic distinctions, 341ab, *Charm.* 163d; he begs Prodicus' pardon (*in absentia*) for riding roughshod over some verbal distinctions (*Meno* 75e), quotes from

would his debt go? A firm answer is impossible, since Prodicus' works are lost to us.[79] But there are two things we can say: first, it would not be fair to Prodicus to assume that his own interest in that distinction would be merely philological. We know that he was a moralist, and, even if we did not, might have inferred it from this very distinction, for the connection of "courage" with "foresight" could not have been squeezed out of ordinary usage; [80] it just was not there to begin with and could only have been made by one who had already decided that it *ought to be* there. But, secondly, after crediting Prodicus with this value judgment, we are still left with the question whether it was not merely *ad hoc* and isolated, but part of an integrated ethical theory and the basis for an extensive revision of current moral appraisals. We have no reason to think that the achievement of Prodicus was of the latter order. In Socrates' case we know that it was. We see his reason for making the distinction in the first place; he deduces it from the premise that "courage is a noble thing," i.e. a moral quality, while confidence, as such, is not.[81] And we know that he exploits its consequences not only, as I have suggested, to raise the moral demands of courage, but also to extend enormously the range of its application. Hitherto it had been mainly the virtue of the *hoplite,* the heavy-armed foot soldier, who had to take the brunt of the bloody and dis- ciplined hand-to-hand fighting of Greek warfare. Socrates now saw how arbitrary was this restriction:

> For I mean to ask you not only about the courage of the heavy infantry but of cavalry-men, too, and of every kind of soldier. And not just of the military, but also of those who are brave in perils at sea, and those who are brave in illness, poverty, or political adversity; and, further still, not only

him the dictum, "the first thing to learn is the right use of words" (*Euthyd.* 277e).

[79] His famous speech on "Heracles at the crossroads" (*ap.* Xenophon, *Mem.* 2.1.21–34) survives only in paraphrase; even so it may be significant that no moral use seems to be made of his linguistic distinctions.

[80] Or etymology: *andreia* (like its Homeric forebear, *ēnoreē*) means "manliness."

[81] 350b; the same point at *Laches* 192cd.

those who face bravely pain or fear, but also those who can be tough in fighting desire or pleasure, holding their ranks or turning against the enemy.[82]

One must stretch one's imagination to see how great an innovation this was. Two generations later, Aristotle concedes it grudgingly and continues to insist that the "first" kind of courage, the one that "most resembles" it (i.e., its only fully adequate instantiation), is that of the citizen soldier,[83] the *hoplite*. So hard it was for Socrates' world to assimilate his thought that courage (as indeed every virtue) is a universal, human norm; that all human beings, even slaves and other base-born persons, could have the noble quality of courage.

CONCLUSION: PROTAGORAS AND SOCRATES

When we are weighing counterclaims we cannot forget those of Protagoras. For him, too, all moral virtues are parts of "human" virtue, "the quality of which all men must be partakers";[1] and by "men" he means 'human beings,' for the effort to teach it extends also to women and children, and, by the same token, why not also to slaves?[2] He gives no quarter to the notion that moral excellence is the special privilege of the genteel, the *kaloi kagathoi*, "the noble and the good" [3]—a phrase which dies hard, survives the advent of democracy, and continues to refer ambiguously to the socially favored and the morally pre-eminent. One of the ideological supports of the moral pretensions of social elites has been the dogma that moral qual-

---

82 *Laches* 191de. The only (partial) parallel is in Democritus (Diels-Kranz, *op. cit.*, 68 B 214; cf. note 70, above).

83 *Nic. Eth.* 1116a 18.

1 325a. The idea is implicit, of course, in his anthropology.

2 That slaves qualify for full-fledged *human* virtue is implicit (and no more) in Protagoras; it comes much closer to explicit mention in Socrates (*Meno* 73d; *Gorg.* 515a).

3 Cf. Socrates' use of it at 347d, translated "real gentlemen."

ities, like physical ones, normally go down from father to son, so may be expected in the offspring of a man of 'quality,' while only by a sport of nature could they turn up in the children of a sausage seller. Some of Protagoras' remarks have ominous implications for this assumption, which was still far from dead in his time. He says that the only qualities it makes sense to blame (or praise) are those which can be produced by "study, exercise, and teaching."[4] From this it would follow that *if* *sophrosynē* and the rest were matters of "nature and of chance"[5] (how damaging for "nature," favorite term of the aristocracy,[6] is its association with "chance"), there would be no sense in making them the objects of moral approval or disapproval, prescription or punishment, just as it makes none to "chastise or instruct the ugly, the diminutive, or the feeble."[7] How clearly Protagoras understands one of the fundamental differences between moral and nonmoral qualities at a time when not even

[4] 323d. Later he says that "courage comes from the nature and good nurture of the soul" (351b), thereby, thinks Taylor (*op. cit.*, p. 258, n. 1) "conceding more importance to *physis* ('original temperament') than we might have expected of him from his earlier utterances." Taylor seems to have forgotten the reference to natural capacities at 327bc (cf. also Diels-Kranz, *op. cit.*, 80 B 3, "teaching needs nature and exercise," one of Protagoras' few surviving fragments). Protagoras' point is obviously that a congenital factor ("nature") is a necessary (though not a sufficient) condition for moral, as for artistic, excellence. This seems sensible enough, though it raises a problem of which he does not seem to be aware: if courage or any other virtue is due partly to "nature," then, on his own theory, (moral) virtue is not wholly a proper object of (moral) blame (or praise). This kind of problem does not seem to have been broached by any Greek moralist. One reason why it did not bother Protagoras was his evident assumption (implied by his remarks at 327c–e) that the differences in natural endowment were relatively small and accounted for a comparatively slight part of moral achievement. Conversely, the proponent of the aristocratic view would also concede "teaching" as one factor in virtue, but think it of little account in comparison with "nature": cf. Pindar, *Nem.* 3.40–43, and W. Jaeger, *Paideia*, I, 2nd ed., New York, 1945, pp. 218–19.

[5] 323de.

[6] Cf. Pindar, *Pyth.* 8.44–45; and look up *phyo, physis* in a Lexicon to Sophocles; a fine example in his *Philoctetes*, at 88–89, with which cf. 79 and 1310–11.

[7] 323d.

a word for "moral" has yet been coined, and one has to get at it by using words like "noble,"[8] though only by forcing them away from their usual, aristocratic connotations. Why then can't Protagoras say that he, too, has humanized, universalized morality? Can't he even say that he has also raised its level, approaching in his own way the high-water mark of classical morality—Socrates' teaching that it is wrong to harm one's enemies? Isn't this the import of Protagoras' doctrine that, except for the rare cases of "incurables," our aim in punishment should be moral improvement?

There is no reason to deny that in all this Protagoras was an exponent of moral enlightenment. Certainly Socrates would not. When he warns Hippocrates of the danger he incurs in associating with a sophist, Socrates does not damn the sophist's offerings *en bloc*. He says that they are a mixed lot, some of them nourishment for the soul, others poison. "If you know which of his wares are good and which are evil, you may safely buy knowledge of Protagoras."[9] If not, not all the fine and wholesome moral truths you might pick up will undo the evil of that one teaching that will be thrust on you, that appearance is all the truth there is. Socrates, as I explained earlier, avoids a head-on attack on this doctrine; for this he would have needed ontological armor which he has long since shed.[10] So

8 *Kalos*, literally 'beautiful'; *gennaios*, literally 'true to one's birth,' and *eugenēs*, 'well-born,' may also be used to mean '(morally) noble, high-minded,' though their currency for this purpose is slight compared to the ubiquitous *kalos, kalon,* and their contraries, *aischros, aischron,* 'base,' literally 'ugly.'

9 313é.

10 All through the modern literature one will find the assumption that there is deep ontological import in his talk of justice, etc., as a "thing" (*pragma*, 330cd, 349b; *chrēmata*, 361b) or "reality" (*ousia*, 349b). But if that is the case, why isn't the issue joined at that point? Why doesn't Protagoras reply to the question, "Is justice some thing or no thing?" 'it isn't a *thing*,' or, better, 'it *is* a thing, and man is its measure' (cf. Part I, Section 3 above)? What is often overlooked is that no particular metaphysical statement need be intended in speaking in Greek of an abstract quality as a "thing"; when the poet Mimnermus (no metaphysician) says (frag. 8), that truth is "the most just thing (*chrēma*) of all," all he is saying is that truth

he shifts the attack to another point, as good, or better, for his purpose: the sovereignty of reason, its power[11] to weigh appearances and judge between them on grounds which, if true for one, are true for all. He asks Protagoras if he, too, thinks of reason as a "noble thing and fit to command in man,"[12] and Protagoras says he does, not realizing how fatal would be the effect of his subjectivism on the claims of reason.[13]

is "more just" than this or that, and one can make no more of the "thing" in Socrates' questions than of "thing" in the English 'anything, something, nothing.' Note that the formal issue between Socrates and Protagoras is not whether each of the virtues is a "thing," but whether or not they are all the *same* "thing"; and the latter can be translated into the question (which wholly avoids *thing*-talk), 'Can a man have one of these virtues without having all the rest at the same time?' *This* is what the argument is all about; when the question is put in this form (329e), Protagoras at last understands it, and responds with the forthright negative which starts off the discussion.

[11] Though he unfortunately confuses 'right to judge' with 'power to make the judgment effective in action,' the root of the mistake discussed in Part II, Section 4, above, over the "absurdity" of *M*. Stating the issue as whether or not "knowledge is a powerful, lordly, commanding thing" (352b) conflates the two notions which (even now) can be conveyed by "power," power in the sense of *ability* and in the quite different sense of *right*.

[12] 352c.

[13] Socrates thereupon takes him at his word and makes him his partner in arguing against the "many," who don't believe this great proposition (our old friend *K*, of Part II, Section 4), and say they don't. Why should Socrates here depart from his usual insistence that his argument must be addressed only to the interlocutor's real opinion? See what he says earlier at 333c, when faced with a similar problem: "My object is to test the validity of the argument [one which Protagoras says he does not share]; and yet the result may be that I who ask and you who answer will both be tested." So here: Protagoras says he believes *K*, and *K* (along with other propositions, including *L* above) implies the contradictory of "the power of appearance." Thus in assenting to *K*, Protagoras is committed to the denial of his subjectivism. But since *L* (the identification of the good and the pleasant) is also used as a premise for this refutation, and Protagoras *repudiates L* (351cd), how is *he* refuted after all? Grube who has a very lucid statement of *this* problem (*Classical Quarterly*, 27, 1933, p. 205), thinks the right answer (p. 206) is that *L* is implied by Protagorean subjectivism. This is surely wrong, since *L* with its "art of measurement" is presented as the "saving principle of life" in *opposition* to subjectivism

Socrates himself is by no means certain as to how these claims are to be made good. In our dialogue he talks, more confidently than he should, as though the "art of measurement,"[14] the arithmetic of pleasure and pain, were the right answer. But if he were asked, 'Are you certain of this?' surely he would reply, 'No; but even if there were nothing better, this would still do as a "saving principle" of human life, a rudder with which to control one's course on the tides of appearance.' Socrates would not impose this "art of measurement" on anyone. He would say, 'Here is the way I got it. Did I make a mistake? Judge for yourself. If you think I did, reason with me, for only by so doing can you show me that my opinion was not just different from yours, but mistaken; not false-for-you-then-and-me-now, but simply false.' Socrates, who renounced certainty for any of his results, might even renounce it for his method of argument, gladly discussing such criticisms as I have made of it above. This would have got him into deeper water than he ever gets into in the Socratic dialogues. But why could he not have braved the journey, so long as there is something to reason about, using reason to find how to use reason better? 'But if we have nothing more than appearances' he might have said to Protagoras, 'there is no basis for deciding what we *should* believe on this or anything else, and none for the validity of our moral convictions, of your view of punishment, or mine of courage, or of our common decision to wrest morality from the arbitrary will of the gods and make of it something which, you say, man's reason has invented, and I say, man's reason can determine and correct.'

As in other Socratic arguments in this one, too, the life of each contestant would be on trial along with his beliefs. The connection is not so simple as Socrates thought it; there is no way to deduce a man's life from his philosophy. But is it an

---

("the power of appearance"). The right answer must be, 'K can only be vindicated on the assumption of L (failing anything better). Protagoras says he agrees to K; therefore, he has to agree to L, unless he could find a way of saying K while dispensing with L.'

14 356de.

accident that of these two men, both of whom were rebels against many of the dogmas that ruled their world, one made all the concessions needed for worldly success, the other conceded nothing, not even when on trial for his life? [15]

GREGORY VLASTOS

[15] I have used in the foregoing more ideas and phrases than I could begin to acknowledge. I trust that the bellicose tone of some of the footnotes will not disguise the fact that the targets of my criticism are, on the whole, the sources from which I have learned the most. Personal thanks are due to my colleagues, C. G. Hempel and H. A. Bedau, for some suggestions; to my wife, Vernon Ladd Vlastos, for many improvements in the style; to the Institute for Advanced Study for enabling me in 1954–55 to do, among other things, the research that lies back of this study.

SELECTED BIBLIOGRAPHY

The books or articles are listed in the order of their usefulness to the beginner.

I. ON PROTAGORAS

Burnet, J., *Greek Philosophy. Thales to Plato,* Ch. VII, "The Sophists." London, 1914.

Sinclair, T. A., *History of Greek Political Thought,* Ch. IV, "Protagoras, the First Great Political Thinker." London, 1951.

Cornford, F. M., *Plato's Theory of Knowledge,* pp. 32–36, 72–74. London, 1935.

Loenen, D., *Protagoras and the Greek Community.* Amsterdam, 1940.

Nestle, W., *Vom Mythos zum Logos,* pp. 264–303. 2nd edition. Stuttgart, 1942.

Kerferd, G. B., "Plato's Doctrine of Justice and Virtue in the *Protagoras,*" *Journal of Hellenic Studies,* LXXIII (1953), 42–45.

————"Plato's Account of the Relativism of Protagoras," *Durham University Journal* (1949), 20–26.

Gomperz, H., *Sophistik und Rhetorik,* Ch. VIII, "Protagoras und die Dialexeis." Leipzig, 1912.

II. ON SOCRATES

Plato, *Euthyphro, Apology, and Crito.*
(Recommended translation: F. J. Church–Robert D. Cumming, "The Library of Liberal Arts" No. 4, New York, 1956.)

Cornford, F. M., *Before and After Socrates,* Ch. II, "Socrates." Cambridge, 1932.

Jaeger, W., *Paideia*, II, Ch. II, "The Memory of Socrates; the Socratic Problem; Socrates the Teacher." Eng. trans. by G. Highet. New York, 1943.

Zeller, E., *Socrates and the Socratic Schools*. Eng. trans. by O. J. Reichel. London, 1868.

Robinson, R., *Plato's Earlier Dialectic*, Chs. II–VI, on "Elenchus," "Epagoge," "Socratic Definition," "Dialectic." 2nd ed. Oxford, 1953.

Snell, B., *The Discovery of the Mind*, Ch. VIII, "The Call to Virtue." Eng. trans. by T. G. Rosenmeyer. Cambridge, Mass., 1953.

Gould, J., *The Development of Plato's Ethics*, Part I, "The Personal Ideal," pp. 3–67. Cambridge, 1955.

Taylor, A. E., *Socrates*. London, 1932.

Maier, H., *Sokrates*. Tübingen, 1913.

III. On Plato's Protagoras

Koyré, A., *Discovering Plato*, pp. 17–33. Eng. trans. by L. C. Rosenfield. New York, 1945.

Grote, G., *Plato*, Ch. XXI. London, 1865.

Taylor, A. E., *Plato*, Ch. X. 6th ed. London, 1949.

Shorey, P., *What Plato Said*, pp. 119–132. Chicago, 1933.

Nestle, W., *Platons Protagoras*. Leipzig, 1931.

Friedländer, P., *Platon*, II, Ch. I. Berlin, 1930.

Woodbury, L., "Simonides on *Arete*," *Transactions of American Philological Association*, LXXXIV (1953), 135–163.

Grube, G. M. A., "The Structural Unity of the *Protagoras*," *Classical Quarterly*, XXVII (1933), 203–207.

Hackforth, R., "Hedonism in Plato's *Protagoras*," *Classical Quarterly*, XXII (1928), 39–42.

PROTAGORAS

PROTAGORAS

CHARACTERS OF THE DIALOGUE

SOCRATES, *who is the narrator of the Dialogue*

HIS COMPANION	PROTAGORAS	
HIPPOCRATES	HIPPIAS	*Sophists*
ALCIBIADES	PRODICUS	
CRITIAS	CALLIAS, *a wealthy Athenian*	

SCENE: *The House of Callias*

1. *Why Go to a Sophist?* (309–314c)

Com. Where do you come from, Socrates? And yet I need St. 309 hardly ask the question, for I know that you have been chasing the prime of youth—the prime of youth of Alcibiades.[1] I saw him the day before yesterday, and he had got a beard like a man—and he is a man, as I may tell you in your ear. But I thought that he was still very charming.

Soc. What of his beard? Are you not of Homer's opinion, who says: "Youth is most charming when the beard first appears"?[2] And that is now the charm of Alcibiades.

Com. Well, and how do matters stand now? Have you been visiting him, and what are his feelings toward you?

Soc. Good, I thought, and especially today, for I have just come from him, and he has been helping me in an argument. But shall I tell you a strange thing? I paid no attention to him, and several times I quite forgot that he was present.

Com. What is the meaning of this? Has anything happened between you and him? For surely you cannot have

[1] [The friendship between Socrates and Alcibiades is well-attested by both Plato and Xenophon, and is perhaps best immortalized through the speech of Alcibiades in Plato's *Symposium*, 215a-222b.]

[2] *Iliad*, XXIV, 348.

3

discovered a fairer love than he is, certainly not in this city of Athens.

Soc. Yes, much fairer.

Com. What do you mean—a citizen or a foreigner?

Soc. A foreigner.

Com. Of what country?

Soc. Of Abdera.

Com. And is this stranger really in your opinion a fairer love than the son of Cleinias?

Soc. And is not the wiser always the fairer, sweet friend?

Com. But have you really met, Socrates, with some wise one?

d   *Soc.* Say rather, with the wisest of all living men, if you are willing to accord that title to Protagoras.

Com. What! Is Protagoras in Athens?

Soc. Yes, he has been here two days.

Com. And do you just come from an interview with him?

310   *Soc.* Yes, and I have said and heard many things.

Com. Then, if you have no engagement, please do sit down right here and tell me about your conversation, and my attendant here shall give up his place to you.

Soc. To be sure; and I shall be grateful to you for listening.

Com. Thank you, too, for telling us.

Soc. That is thank you twice over. Listen then.

Last night, or rather very early this morning, Hippocrates, the son of Apollodorus and the brother of Phason,[3]
b gave a tremendous thump with his staff at my door. Someone opened to him, and he came rushing in and bawled out: Socrates, are you awake or asleep?

I recognized his voice, and said: Hippocrates, is that you? No bad news, I hope?

Good news, he said, nothing but good.

Delightful, I said; but what is the news? And why have you come here at this unearthly hour?

He drew nearer to me and said: Protagoras has arrived.

---

[3] [Apart from his appearance in this dialogue, nothing is known about this Hippocrates.]

Yes, I replied. He came two days ago; have you only just heard of his arrival?

Yes, by the gods, he said, but not until yesterday evening.

At the same time he felt for the truckle bed and sat down   c
at my feet, and then he said: Yesterday quite late in the evening, on my return from Oenoe. I had gone there in pursuit of my runaway slave Satyrus, as I meant to have told you if some other matter had not come in the way. On my return, when after supper we were about to retire to rest, my brother said to me: Protagoras has arrived. I was going to you at once, and then I thought that the night was far spent. But the moment sleep left me after my fatigue, I got up and came straight   d
here.

I who knew the eagerness and excitement of the man said: What is that to you? Has Protagoras robbed you of something?

He replied, laughing: Yes, indeed, he has, Socrates, of the wisdom which he keeps from me.

But surely, I said, if you give him money and talk him into it, he will make you wise, too.

Would to heaven, he replied, that it depended on that! He might take all that I have, and all that my friends have,   e
if he pleased. But that is why I have come to you now, in order that you may speak to him on my behalf, for I am young, and also I have never seen nor heard him (when he visited Athens before I was but a child),[4] and all men praise him, Socrates; he is reputed to be the most accomplished of speakers. There is no reason why we should not go to him at once, so that we shall find him at home. He lodges, as I hear,   311
with Callias, the son of Hipponicus[5]; let us go.

[4] [It was probably on his earlier visit in 445 B.C. that Protagoras was entrusted by Pericles with drawing up a constitution for the Pan-Hellenic colony sent to Thurii in Southern Italy.]

[5] [Callias (ca. 450-370 B.C.) was a member of one of the richest and oldest noble families at Athens, who traditionally held one of the important priesthoods at Eleusis. He was notorious for his extravagance and his passion for the Sophists. The scene of Xenophon's *Symposium* is also laid at his house.]

I replied: Not yet, my good friend, the hour is too early. But let us rise and take a turn in the court and wait about there until daybreak. When the day breaks, then we will go. For Protagoras is usually at home, and we shall be sure to find him in, never fear.

b Upon this we got up and walked about in the court, and I thought that I would test the strength of his resolution. So I examined him and put questions to him. Tell me, Hippocrates, I said, as you are going to Protagoras and will be paying your money to him, what is he to whom you are going and what will he make of you? If, for example, you had thought of going to Hippocrates of Cos, the Asclepiad, and were about to give him your money, and someone had said to you: You are paying money to your namesake Hippocrates, O Hippocrates; tell me, what is he that you give him

c money? How would you have answered?

I should say, he replied, that I gave money to him as a physician.

And what will he make of you?

A physician, he said.

And if you were resolved to go to Polycleitus the Argive, or Pheidias the Athenian, and were intending to give them money, and someone had asked you: What are Polycleitus and Pheidias, and why do you propose to give them this money? How would you have answered?

I should have answered that they were sculptors.

And what will they make of you?

A sculptor, of course.

d Well now, I said, you and I are going to Protagoras, and we are ready to pay him money as a fee on your behalf. If our own means are sufficient and we can gain him with these, we shall be only too glad; but if not, then we are to spend the money of your friends as well. Now suppose that, while we are thus enthusiastically pursuing our object, someone were to say to us: Tell me, Socrates, and you, Hippocrates,

e what is Protagoras, and why do you propose to pay him money? How should we answer? I know that Pheidias is a sculptor, and that Homer is a poet, but what appellation is given to Protagoras? How is he designated?

They call him a Sophist, Socrates, he replied.

Then we are going to pay our money to him in the character of a Sophist?

Certainly.

But suppose a person were to ask you this further question: And how about yourself? What will Protagoras make of you if you go to see him? 312

He answered, with a blush upon his face (for the day was just beginning to dawn, so that I could see him): Unless this differs in some way from the former instances, I suppose that he will make a Sophist of me.

By the gods, I said, and would you not be ashamed to present yourself to the Hellenes in the character of a Sophist?

Indeed, Socrates, to confess the truth, I am.

But surely you mean, Hippocrates, that the instruction you will receive from Protagoras will not be of this nature, but rather that it will be like the instruction you have received when you got your elementary schooling, your lyre lessons, and your physical training. For you learned all that not in order to acquire a professional skill which you would practice as a specialist, but to get an education as befits a layman and a freeman. b

Just so, he said. And that, in my opinion, is a far truer account of the teaching of Protagoras.

I said: I wonder whether you know what you are doing.

And what am I doing?

You are going to commit your soul to the care of a man whom you call a Sophist. And yet I hardly think that you know what a Sophist is; and if not, then you do not even know to whom you are committing your soul and whether the thing to which you commit yourself be good or evil. c

I certainly think that I do know, he replied.

Then tell me what do you imagine a Sophist is?

I take him to be one who knows wise things, he replied, as his name implies.

And might you not, I said, affirm this of the painter and of the carpenter also? Do not they, too, know wise things? But

d suppose a person were to ask us: In what wise things are the painters knowledgeable? We should answer: In what relates to the making of likenesses. And similarly of other things. And if he were further to ask: In what branch of wisdom is the Sophist knowledgeable, and what is the manufacture over which he presides—how should we answer him?

How should we answer him, Socrates? What other answer could there be but that he presides over the art which makes men eloquent?

Yes, I replied, that is very likely true, but not enough, for the answer begs the further question: Of what does the Sophist make a man talk eloquently? The player on the lyre

e may be supposed to make a man talk eloquently about that which he makes him understand—that is, about playing the lyre. Is not that true?

Yes.

Then about what does the Sophist make him eloquent? Must not he make him eloquent in that which he understands?

Yes, that may be assumed.

And what is that which the Sophist knows and makes his disciple know?

Indeed, he said, I cannot tell.

313 Then I proceeded to say: Well, but are you aware of the danger which you are running in submitting your soul to him? If you were going to commit your body to someone who might do good or harm to it, would you not carefully consider and ask the opinion of your friends and kindred, and deliberate many days as to whether or not you should give him the care of your body? But when the soul is in question, which you hold to be of far more value than the body, and upon the good or evil of which depends the well-being of your all—then you never consulted either with your father or with your

b brother or with anyone of us who are your companions whether or not you should commit your own soul to this foreigner who has come. In the evening, as you say, you hear of

him, and in the morning you go to him, never deliberating
or taking the opinion of anyone as to whether you ought to
entrust yourself to him or not. You have quite made up your
mind that you must by hook or by crook be a pupil of Protagoras, and are prepared to expend all the property of yourself
and of your friends in carrying out this determination, although, as you admit, you do not know him and have never
spoken with him; and you call him a Sophist, but are mani- c
festly ignorant of what a Sophist is; and yet you are going to
commit yourself to his keeping.

When he heard me say this, he replied: No other inference, Socrates, can be drawn from your words.

I proceeded: Is not a Sophist, Hippocrates, a person who
deals wholesale or retail in such wares as provide food for the
soul? I for one think that that is the kind of person he is.

And what, Socrates, is the food of the soul?

Surely, I said, knowledge is the food of the soul; and we
must take care, my friend, that the Sophist does not deceive
us when he praises what he sells, like the dealers, wholesale d
or retail, who sell the food of the body, for they praise indis-
criminately all their goods without knowing what is really
beneficial or hurtful for the body. Neither do their customers
know, with the exception of a trainer or physician who
may happen to buy of them. In like manner those who carry
about the wares of knowledge and make the round of the
cities and offer or retail them to any customer who wants
them, praise them all alike, though I should not be surprised,
my dear fellow, if some of them, too, did not know which of
their goods have a good and which a bad effect upon the soul;
and their customers are equally ignorant, unless he who buys e
of them happens to be a physician of the soul. If you know
which of his wares are good and which are evil, you may safely
buy knowledge of Protagoras or of anyone; but if not, then,
my friend, watch out, don't take risks, don't gamble, with the
most precious thing you have. For there is far greater risk in 314
buying knowledge than in buying food and drink. The one
you purchase of the wholesale or retail dealer, and carry them

away in other vessels, and before you receive them into the body as food or drink, you may deposit them at home and call in an expert to give you advice—who knows what is good
b   to be eaten and drunk, and what not, and how much, and when; and then the risk of purchasing them is not so great. But you cannot buy knowledge and carry it away in another vessel; when you have paid for it you must receive it into the soul and go on your way, either greatly harmed or greatly benefited. These things let us investigate with our elders, for we are still young—too young to determine such a matter. And now let us go, as we were intending, and hear Protagoras; and when we have heard what he has to say, we may impart it to others. For not only is Protagoras at the house of Callias,
c   but there is Hippias of Elis[6], and, if I am not mistaken, Prodicus of Ceos[7] and several other wise men.

2. Protagoras Explains his Calling (314c–319a)

To this we agreed and proceeded on our way until we reached the vestibule of the house, and there we stopped in order to conclude, before entering the house, a discussion which had arisen between us as we were going along, and we stood talking in the vestibule until we had finished and come to an understanding. And I think that the doorkeeper, who was a eunuch and who was probably annoyed at the great in-
d   road of the Sophists, must have heard us talking. At any rate, when we knocked at the door and he opened and saw us, he grumbled: They are Sophists—he is not at home; and instantly gave the door a hearty bang with both his hands.

[6] [Hippias of Elis (ca. 481-411 B.C.) was a widely traveled Sophist and polymath, especially famed for his contributions to mathematics and to chronology, the latter through a compilation of a complete list of the victors at the Olympic Games.]

[7] [Prodicus of Ceos, whose exact dates are not known, was a Sophist whose particular interest was the study of the meaning of words. That he also concerned himself with ethical problems is attested by the story of the "Choice of Heracles" which Xenophon, Memorabilia, II, i, 21-34, attributes to him.]

Again we knocked, and he answered, without opening: Did you not hear me say that he is not at home, fellows? But, my friend, I said, you need not be alarmed, for we are not Sophists, and we did not come to see Callias, but we do want to see Protagoras, and I must request you to announce us. At last, after a good deal of difficulty, the man was persuaded to open the door.

e

When we entered, we found Protagoras taking a walk in the cloister; and attending him in proper order on one side were walking Callias, the son of Hipponicus, and Paralus, the son of Pericles, who by the mother's side is his half-brother,[8] and Charmides, the son of Glaucon.[9] On the other side of him were Xanthippus, the other son of Pericles, Philippides, the son of Philomelus; also Antimoerus of Mende,[10] who of all the disciples of Protagoras is the most famous and intends to make sophistry his profession. A train of listeners followed him. The greater part of them appeared to be foreigners, whom Protagoras always brings with him out of the various cities visited by him in his journeys—he, like Orpheus, charming them with his voice, and they following its spell. I should mention also that there were some Athenians in the chorus. Nothing delighted me more than the spectacle of this chorus and the punctilious care they took never to get into Protagoras' way. But whenever he and those who were with him turned back, then the band of listeners parted regularly on either side, wheeled around, and took their places behind him in perfect order.

315

b

After him, as Homer says, "I lifted up my eyes and saw" [11]

8 [The mother of Callias later became the wife of Pericles to whom she bore Xanthippus and Paralus.]

9 [Charmides was the brother of Plato's mother, i.e., Plato's uncle. Like Critias (Plato's cousin once removed) he was associated with the regime of horror that ruled Athens after the end of the Peloponnesian War.]

10 [Practically nothing outside this passage is known of Philippides and Antimoerus.]

11 [*Odyssey*, XI, 601.]

c Hippias the Elean sitting in the opposite cloister on a chair of state, and around him were seated on benches Eryximachus, the son of Acumenus,[12] and Phaedrus the Myrrhinusian,[13] and Andron, the son of Androtion,[14] and there were strangers both from his native Elis, and some others; they were putting to Hippias certain physical and astronomical questions and he, *ex cathedra,* was passing judgment upon their several questions and discussing them.

Also "my eyes beheld Tantalus," [15] for Prodicus the Cean
d was at Athens, too; he had been lodged in a room which, in the days of Hipponicus, was a storehouse; but, as the house was full, Callias had cleared this out and made the room into a guest room. Now Prodicus was still in bed, wrapped up in sheepskins and bedclothes, of which there seemed to be a great heap; and there was sitting near by him on the couches Pausanias of the deme of Cerameis; [16] and with Pausanias was a youth quite young, who is certainly remarkable for his good
e looks and, if I am not mistaken, is also of a fair and gentle nature. I thought that I heard him called Agathon,[17] and my suspicion is that he is the beloved of Pausanias. There was this youth, and also there were the two Adeimantuses, one the son of Cepis, and the other of Leucolophides,[18] and some

[12] [Eryximachus was a physician and a member of the Athenian intelligentsia, who also participates in Plato's *Symposium.*]

[13] [Phaedrus' penchant for the Sophists and rhetoric is well known from the Platonic dialogue named after him. He also initiates the discussion of love in the *Symposium.*]

[14] [Andron is also mentioned in the *Gorgias* (487c) as a student of philosophy. He may have been the father of the fourth-century orator and historian Androtion.]

[15] [*Odyssey*, XI, 582.]

[16] [Pausanias is one of the interlocutors both in Plato's and in Xenophon's *Symposium,* where reference is also made to his love for Agathon.]

[17] [Agathon is the elegant, sophisticated, and somewhat effeminate tragic poet, in whose honor and at whose house Plato's *Symposium* takes place.]

[18] [Nothing is known of the son of Cepis. The son of Leucolophides was a general with Alcibiades in the expedition against Andros in 407 B.C. and was again appointed to that office after the battle of the Arginusae,

others. I was very anxious to hear what Prodicus was saying, **316**
for he seems to me to be an all-wise and inspired man; but I
was not able to get into the inner circle, and his deep voice
made an echo in the room which rendered his words inaudible.

No sooner had we entered than there followed us Alcibiades the beautiful, as you say, and I believe you, and also
Critias, the son of Callaeschrus.[19]

On entering we stopped a little in order to look about
us, and then walked up to Protagoras, and I said: Protagoras,   **b**
my friend Hippocrates here and I have come to see you.

Do you wish, he said, to speak with me alone or in the
presence of the company?

Whichever you please, I said; you shall determine when
you have heard the purpose of our visit.

And what is your purpose? he said.

I must explain, I said, that my friend Hippocrates is a
native Athenian. He is the son of Apollodorus, and of a great
and prosperous house, and he is himself in natural ability
regarded as quite a match for anybody of his own age. I believe that he aspires to political eminence, and he thinks that   **c**
association with you is most likely to procure this for him.
And now you can determine whether you would wish to speak
to him of your teaching alone or in the presence of the
company.

Thank you, Socrates, for your consideration of me. For
certainly a foreigner finding his way into great cities, and
persuading the flower of youth in them to leave the company of others, kinsmen or strangers, old or young, and live
with him, under the idea that they will be improved by their
association with him, ought to be very cautious. Great jealous-   **d**
ies are aroused by his proceedings, and he is the subject of

---

continuing in that office until the Athenian defeat at Aegospotami in 405
B.C. In that battle he was taken prisoner and, unlike his colleagues, was
not put to death by the Spartans.]

19 [Critias (ca. 460-403 B.C.) was a poet of sorts and became the leader
of the notorious Thirty Tyrants after the end of the Peloponnesian War.
On his relation to Plato, see note 9 on Charmides.]

Sophists

many enmities and conspiracies. Now the art of the Sophist is, as I believe, of great antiquity, but in ancient times those who practiced it, fearing this odium, veiled and disguised themselves under various names, some under those of poets, as Homer, Hesiod, and Simonides; some of mystic initiates and prophets, as Orpheus and Musaeus; and some, as I observe, even under the name of gymnastic masters, like Iccus of Tarentum, or the more recently celebrated Herodicus, now of

e   Selymbria and formerly of Megara, who is a first-rate Sophist. Your own Agathocles pretended to be a musician, but was really an eminent Sophist; also Pythocleides the Cean; and there were many others. All of them, as I was saying, adopted these arts as veils or disguises because they were afraid of the odium they would incur. But that is not my way, for I do not

317 believe that they effected their purpose. The authorities in the various cities did not fail to see through their pretense. And as for the people, they have no understanding and only repeat what their leaders are pleased to tell them. Now to run away without being able to make good one's escape and to get

b   caught is a great folly, and it invariably increases the enmity of mankind. For in addition to his other shortcomings they regard the runaway as a desperado. Therefore, I take an entirely opposite course and acknowledge myself to be a Sophist and instructor of mankind. Such an open acknowledgment appears to me to be a better sort of caution than concealment. Nor do I neglect other precautions, and therefore I hope, as I may say, by the favor of heaven that no harm will come of

c   the acknowledgment that I am a Sophist. And I have been now many years in the profession—for all my years when added up are many. There is no one here present of whom, in terms of age, I might not be the father. Wherefore I should much prefer conversing with you about all that, if you want to speak with me, in the presence of the company inside.

As I suspected that he would like to have a little display and glorification in the presence of Prodicus and Hippias, and would gladly show us to them in the light of admirers, I

said: But why should we not summon Prodicus and Hippias   d
and their friends to hear us?

Very good, he said.

Suppose, said Callias, that we stage a regular meeting in
which you may sit and discuss. This was agreed upon, and
great delight was felt at the prospect of hearing wise men
talk; we ourselves took the benches and couches and arranged
them by Hippias, where the other benches had been already
placed. Meanwhile Callias and Alcibiades got Prodicus out
of bed and brought in him and his companions.   e

When we were all seated, Protagoras said: Now that the
company is assembled, Socrates, tell me about the young man
of whom you were just now speaking.

I replied: I will begin again at the same point, Protagoras,   318
and tell you once more the purport of my visit. This is my
friend Hippocrates, who is desirous of making your acquaintance. He would like to know what will happen to him if he
associates with you. I have no more to say.

Protagoras answered: Young man, if you associate with
me, on the very first day you will be in a position to return
home a better man than you came, and better on the second
day than on the first, and better every day than you were on
the day before.

When I heard this, I said: Protagoras, I do not at all won-   b
der at hearing you say this; even at your age, and with all
your wisdom, if anyone were to teach you what you did not
know before, you would become better, no doubt. But please
answer in a different way—I will explain how by an example.
Let me suppose that Hippocrates, instead of desiring your
acquaintance, wished to become acquainted with the young
man Zeuxippus of Heraclea,[20] who has lately been in Athens,
and he had come to him as he has come to you, and had heard
him say, as he has heard you say, that every day he would   c

20 [Zeuxippus, better known by his shortened name Zeuxis, lived in
the last half of the fifth century B.C. and was one of the most celebrated
painters of classical antiquity.]

grow and become better if he associated with him; and then suppose that he were to ask him, "In what shall I become better, and in what shall I grow?" Zeuxippus would answer, "In painting." And suppose that he went to Orthagoras the Theban, and heard him say the same thing you said, and asked him, "In what shall I become better day by day if I associate with you?" He would reply, "In flute playing." Now I want you to make the same sort of answer to this young man and to me, who am asking questions on his account. When you say that on the first day on which Hippocrates associates

d with Protagoras he will return home a better man, and on every day will grow in like manner—in what, Protagoras, will he be better, and about what?

When Protagoras heard me say this he replied: You ask good questions, Socrates, and I like to answer a question which is well put. If Hippocrates comes to me he will not experience the sort of drudgery with which other Sophists are in the habit of insulting their pupils who, when they have

e just escaped from the arts, are taken and driven back into them by these teachers, and made to learn calculation, and astronomy, and geometry, and music (he gave a look at Hippias as he said this). But if he comes to me, he will learn only that which he comes to learn. And this is prudence in affairs private as well as public; he will learn to order his

319 own house in the best manner, and he will be able to speak and act most powerfully in the affairs of the state.

Do I understand you, I said, and is your meaning that you teach the art of politics, and that you promise to make men good citizens?

That, Socrates, is exactly the profession which I make.

3. Can Virtue be Taught? (319a–320c)

Then, I said, you possess a noble art, indeed, if you really do possess it. For I will freely confess to you, Protagoras, that I have a doubt whether this art is capable of

b being taught, and yet I know not how to disbelieve your assertion. And I ought to tell you why I am of opinion that this art cannot be taught or communicated by man to man. I say that the Athenians are a wise people, and indeed they are esteemed to be such by the other Hellenes. Now I observe that when we are met together in the Assembly, and the matter in hand relates to building, the builders are summoned as advisers; when the question is one of shipbuilding, then the shipwrights; and the like of other arts which they think capable of being taught and learned. And if some person offers to give them advice who is not supposed by them to be an expert craftsman, even though he be good-looking and rich and noble, they will not listen to him, but laugh and hoot at him until either he is clamored down and retires of himself, or, if he persists, he is dragged away or put out by the constables at the command of the prytanes.[21] This is their way of behaving about specialists in the arts. But when the question concerns an affair of state, then everybody is free to get up and give advice—carpenter, tinker, cobbler, passenger and shipowner, rich and poor, high and low—and no one reproaches him, as in the former case, with not having learned and having no teacher, and yet giving advice; evidently, because they are under the impression that this sort of knowledge cannot be taught. And not only is this true of the state, but of individuals. The best and wisest of our citizens are unable to impart their political wisdom to others; as, for example, Pericles, the father of these young men, who gave them excellent instruction in all that could be learned from masters; in his own department of politics he neither taught them nor gave them teachers, but they were allowed to wander at their own free will in a sort of hope that they would light upon virtue of their own accord. Or take another example. There was Cleinias, the younger brother of our friend Alcibiades, of whom this very same Pericles was the guardian. And he being in fact under the apprehension that Cleinias would be corrupted by Alcibiades, took him away and placed

c

d

e

320

---

[21] [The prytanes constituted the executive committee of the Council of the Five Hundred.]

him in the house of Ariphron to be educated. But before six months had elapsed, Ariphron sent him back, not knowing
b   what to do with him. And I could mention numberless other instances of persons who were good themselves, and never yet made anyone else good, whether a member of their family or a stranger. Now I, Protagoras, having these examples before me, am inclined to think that virtue cannot be taught. But then again, when I listen to your words I waver and am disposed to think that there must be something in what you say, because I believe that you have great experience and learning and invention. And I wish that you would, if possible, show
c   me a little more clearly that virtue can be taught. Will you be so good?

4. _Protagoras' Great Speech_ (320c–328d)

That I will, Socrates, and gladly. But what would you like? Shall I, as an elder, tell you as younger men a myth, or shall I argue out the question?

To this several of the company answered that he should choose for himself.

Well then, he said, I think that the myth will be more interesting.

Once upon a time there were gods only, and no mortal
d   creatures. But when the destined time came that these also should be created, the gods fashioned them out of earth and fire and various mixtures of both elements in the interior of the earth. And when they were about to bring them into the light of day, they ordered Prometheus and Epimetheus[22] to equip them and to distribute to them severally their proper qualities. Epimetheus begged Prometheus: "Let me distribute, and do you inspect." Prometheus agreed, and Epimetheus made the distribution. There were some to whom he gave strength without swiftness, while he equipped the weaker with
e   swiftness; some he armed, and others he left unarmed, and

22 [Prometheus is derived from the word meaning "forethought" and Epimetheus from "afterthought."]

devised for the latter some other means of preservation, making some large and having their size as a protection, and others small, whose nature was to fly in the air or burrow in the ground; this was to be their way of escape. Thus did he compensate them with the view of preventing any race from becoming extinct. And when he had made sufficient provision against their destruction by one another, he contrived also a means of protecting them against the seasons that come from Zeus, clothing them with close hair and thick skins sufficient to defend them against the winter cold and able to resist the summer heat, so that they might have a natural bed of their own when they wanted to rest. Also he furnished them with hoofs and hard and callous skins under their feet. Then he gave them varieties of food—herb of the soil to some, to others fruits of trees, and to others roots, and to some again he gave other animals as food. And some he made to have few young ones, while those who were their prey were very prolific. And in this manner the race was preserved. Thus did Epimetheus, not being very wise, forget that he had distributed among the brute animals all the qualities which he had to give. And when he came to the race of men, which was still unprovided, he did not know what to do. Now while he was in this perplexity, Prometheus came to inspect the distribution, and he found that the other animals were suitably furnished, but that man alone was naked and shoeless, and had neither bed nor arms of defense. The appointed hour was approaching when man in his turn was to go forth from the earth into the light of day. And Prometheus, not knowing how he could devise man's preservation, stole the wisdom of practicing the arts of Hephaestus and Athene, and fire with it (it could neither have been acquired nor used without fire), and gave them to man. Thus man had the wisdom necessary to the support of life, but political wisdom he had not, for that was in the keeping of Zeus. There was no longer any time for Prometheus to enter into the citadel of heaven where Zeus dwelt, who, moreover, had terrible sentinels. But he did enter by stealth into the common workshop of Athene and He-

321

b

c

d

e   phaestus in which they used to practice their favorite arts,
     and carried off Hephaestus' art of working by fire, and also
     the art of Athene, and gave them to man. And in this way
     man was well supplied with the means of life. But Prometheus
322 is said to have been afterward prosecuted for theft, owing to
     the blunder of Epimetheus.

          Now man, having a share in divinity, was at first the only
     one of the animals who had any gods, because he alone was
     of their kindred, and he would raise altars and images of
     them. He was not long in inventing articulate speech and
     names; and he also constructed houses and clothes and shoes
     and beds, and drew sustenance from the earth. Thus provided,
b   mankind at first lived dispersed, and there were no cities. But
     the consequence was that they were destroyed by the wild
     beasts, for they were utterly weak in comparison to them, and
     their arts and crafts were only sufficient to provide them with
     the means of life, and did not enable them to carry on war
     against the brutes. Food they had, but not as yet the art of
     government, of which the art of war is a part. After a while
     the desire of collective living and of self-preservation made
     them found cities; but when they were gathered together, hav-
     ing no art of government, they dealt unjustly with one an-
     other, and were again in process of dispersion and destruc-
c   tion. Zeus feared that our entire race would be exterminated,
     and so he sent Hermes to mankind, bearing reverence and
     justice to be the ordering principles of cities and the uniting
     bonds of friendship. Hermes asked Zeus how he should im-
     part justice and reverence among men: "Shall I distribute
     them as the arts are distributed; that is to say, to a few only,
     one specialist in the art of medicine or in any other art being
     sufficient for a large number of laymen? Shall this be the man-
     ner in which I am to distribute justice and reverence among
d   men, or shall I give them to all?" "To all," said Zeus, "I
     should like them all to have a share; for cities cannot exist
     if a few only share in justice and reverence, as in the arts.
     And further, make a law by my order that he who has no part

in reverence and justice shall be put to death, for he is a plague of the state."

And this is the reason, Socrates, why the Athenians, and mankind in general, when the question relates to excellence in carpentry or any other mechanical art, allow but a few to share in their deliberations. And when anyone else interferes, then, as you say, they object if he be not of the few; which, as I reply, is very natural. But when they meet to deliberate about political excellence or virtue, which proceeds only by way of justice and self-control, they are patient enough of any man who speaks of them, as is also natural, because they think that every man ought to share in this sort of virtue, and that states could not exist if this were otherwise. I have explained to you, Socrates, the reason of this phenomenon.

And that you may not suppose yourself to be deceived in thinking that all men actually do regard every man as having a share of justice and of every other political virtue, let me give you a further proof, which is this. In other cases, as you are aware, if a man says that he is a good flute-player, or skillful in any other art in which he has no skill, people either laugh at him or are angry with him, and his relations think that he is mad and go and admonish him. But when justice is in question, or some other political virtue, even if they know that he is unjust, yet, if the man of his own accord comes publicly forward and tells the truth, then, what in the other case was held by them to be good sense, i.e., to tell the truth, they now deem to be madness. They say that all men ought to profess justice whether they are just or not, and that a man is out of his mind who says anything else. Their notion is that a man must have some degree of justice, and that if he has none at all he ought not to be in human society.

I have been showing that they are right in admitting every man as a counselor about this sort of virtue, as they are of opinion that every man is a partaker of it. And I will now endeavor to show further that they do not conceive this virtue to be given by nature, or to grow spontaneously, but to

be a thing which is taught, and which comes to a man by taking pains. No one would instruct, no one would rebuke or be
angry with those whose calamities they suppose to be due to
d nature or chance; they do not try to punish or to prevent
them from being what they are; they do but pity them. Who,
for example, is so foolish as to chastise or instruct the ugly,
the diminutive, or the feeble? And for this reason: because he
knows that good and evil of this kind is the work of nature
and of chance, whereas if a man is wanting in those good
qualities which are attained by study and exercise and teach-
e ing, and has only the contrary evil qualities, other men are
angry with him, and punish and reprove him. Of these evil
qualities one is injustice, another impiety; and they may be
324 described generally as the very opposite of political virtue.
In such cases any man will be angry with another and repri-
mand him—clearly because he thinks that by study and learning the virtue in which the other is deficient may be acquired.
If you will think, Socrates, of what punishment can do for
the evildoer, you will see at once that in the opinion of mankind virtue may be acquired. No one punishes the evildoer
under the notion, or for the reason, that he has done wrong—
b only the unreasonable fury of a beast is so vindictive. But he
who desires to inflict rational punishment does not punish
for the sake of a past wrong which cannot be undone; he has
regard to the future and is desirous that the man who is
punished, and he who sees him punished, may be deterred
from doing wrong again. He punishes for the sake of prevention, thereby clearly implying that virtue is capable of
being taught. This is the notion of all who punish others
c either privately or publicly. And the Athenians, especially,
your fellow citizens no less than other men, punish and correct all whom they regard as evildoers. And hence we may
infer them to be of the number of those who think that virtue
may be acquired and taught. Thus far, Socrates, I have shown
you clearly enough, if I am not mistaken, that your country-
men are right in admitting the tinker and the cobbler to ad-

Enlightened views of punishment

vise about politics, and also that they deem virtue to be capa-
ble of being taught and acquired.   d

There yet remains one problem which has been raised by
you about the sons of good men. What is the reason why good
men teach their sons the knowledge which is gained from
teachers, and make them wise in that, but do nothing toward
improving them in the virtues which distinguish themselves?
And here, Socrates, I will leave the myth and resume the argument. Please consider: is there or is there not some one
quality of which all the citizens must be partakers if there is
to be a city at all? In the answer to this question is contained   e
the only solution of your difficulty; there is no other. For if
there be any such quality, and this one thing is not the art of
the carpenter, or the smith, or the potter, but justice and
self-control and piety and, in a word, human virtue—if this is   325
the quality of which all men must be partakers, and which is
the very condition of their learning or doing anything else,
and if he who is wanting in this, whether he be a child or an
adult man or woman, must be taught and punished until by
punishment he becomes better, and he who rebels against instruction and punishment is either exiled from the city or con-
demned to death under the idea that he is incurable—if what   b
I am saying be true, good men have their sons taught other
things and not this, do consider how extraordinary their conduct would appear to be. For we have shown that they think
virtue capable of being taught both in private and public. But
though it can be taught and cultivated, they have their sons
taught lesser matters ignorance of which does not involve the
death penalty. But greater things of which ignorance may cause
death or exile to their children if these have no training in or
knowledge of virtue—aye, confiscation as well as death and,   c
in a word, the ruin of families—those things, I say, they are
supposed not to teach them, not to take the utmost care that
they should learn. How improbable is this, Socrates!

Education and admonition commence in the first years of
childhood, and last to the very end of life. Mother and nurse

d   and father and tutor are vying with one another about the
improvement of the child as soon as ever he is able to understand what is being said to him; he cannot say or do anything without their setting forth to him that this is just and
that is unjust; this is noble, that is base; this is pious, that is
impious; do this and don't do that. And if he willingly obeys,
well and good. If not, he is straightened by threats and blows,
like a piece of bent or warped wood. At a later stage they
send him to teachers, and enjoin them to see to his manners
e   even more than to his reading and music; and the teachers
do as they are asked. And when the boy has learned his letters
and is beginning to understand what is written, as before he
understood only what was spoken, they put into his hands
the works of great poets, which he reads sitting on a bench
326   at school. In these are contained many admonitions, and
many tales, and praises, and encomia of ancient, famous men,
which he is required to learn by heart in order that he may
imitate or emulate them and desire to become like them.
Then, again, the teachers of the lyre take similar care that
their young disciple is self-controlled and gets into no mis-
chief. And when they have taught him the use of the lyre, they
introduce him to the poems of other excellent poets, who are
the lyric poets; and these they set to music, and make their
b   harmonies and rhythms quite familiar to the children's souls,
in order that they may learn to be more gentle, and harmonious, and rhythmical, and so more fitted for speech and action,
for the life of man in every part has need of harmony and
rhythm. Then they send them to the master of gymnastics, in
order that their bodies may better minister to the sound
c   mind, and that they may not be compelled through bodily
weakness to play the coward in war or on any other occasion. And the more socially influential people are, the more
they go in for that, and the richest are the most influential.
Their children begin to go to school soonest and leave off
latest. When they have done with masters, the state again
compels them to learn the laws and live after the pattern
d   which they furnish, and not after their own fancies; and just

as in learning to write the writing master first draws lines
with a style for the use of the young beginner, and gives him
the tablet and makes him follow the lines, so the city draws
the laws, which were the invention of good lawgivers living in
the olden time, and compels the young man to rule and be
ruled in accordance with them. He who transgresses them is
to be corrected or, in other words, called to account, which is
a term used not only in your country, but also in many others,
seeing that justice calls men to account. Now when there is   e
all this care about virtue, private and public, why, Socrates,
do you still wonder and doubt whether virtue can be taught?
Cease to wonder, for it would be far more surprising if it
were not teachable.

But why then do the sons of good fathers often turn out
ill? I'll tell you. There is nothing very wonderful in this, for
if I have been right in what I have been saying, a state can
exist only if everyone is an expert in this thing, virtue. If so—   327
and nothing can be truer—then I will further ask you to
imagine, as an illustration, some other pursuit or branch of
knowledge which may be assumed equally to be the condition
of the existence of a state. Suppose that there could be no
state unless we were all flute-players, as far as each had the
capacity, and everybody was teaching everybody the art, both
in private and public, and reproving the bad player as freely
and openly as every man now teaches justice and the laws, not
concealing them as he would conceal the other arts, but im-   b
parting them—for all of us profit from each other's justice
and virtue, and this is the reason why everyone is so ready to
teach anyone justice and the laws—suppose, I say, that there
were the same readiness and liberality among us in teaching
one another flute-playing, do you imagine, Socrates, that the
sons of good flute-players would be more likely to be good
than the sons of bad ones? I think not. Their sons grow up
to be distinguished or undistinguished according to their own
natural capacities as flute-players, and the son of a good   c
player would often turn out to be a bad one, and the son of a
bad player to be a good one, and all flute-players would be

good enough in comparison with those who were ignorant and unacquainted with the art of flute-playing. In like manner I would have you now consider that he who appears to you to be the most unjust of those who have been brought up in laws and society would appear to be a just man and a master of justice if he were to be compared with men who had no edu-

d   cation, or courts of justice, or laws, or any restraints upon them which compelled them to practice virtue—with the savages, for example, whom the poet Pherecrates exhibited on the stage at last year's Lenaean festival.[23] If you were living among men such as the man-haters in his Chorus, you would be only too glad to meet with Eurybatus and Phrynondas,[24] and you would sorrowfully long to revisit the rascality of this part of the world. So you are actually living a life

e   of luxury, Socrates, and the reason is that all men are teachers of virtue, each one according to his ability. And you say: Where are the teachers? You might as well ask, Who teaches

328   Greek? For of that, too, there will not be any teachers found. Or you might ask, Who is to teach the sons of our artisans this same art which they have learned of their fathers? The father and his fellow workmen have taught them to the best of their ability, but who will carry them further in their arts? And you would certainly have a difficulty, Socrates, in finding a teacher of them; but there would be no difficulty in finding a teacher of those who are wholly ignorant. And this is true of virtue or of anything else. If a man is better able than we

b   are to promote virtue ever so little, we must be content with the result. A teacher of this sort I believe myself to be, and above all other men help people attain what is noble and good; and I give my pupils their money's worth and even

---

[23] [Pherecrates (*fl. ca.* 430-410 B.C.), a poet of the Old Comedy, is said to have produced a play, entitled *The Savages*, in 421/0 B.C. Though this is doubtless the play referred to here, its date does not tally with the dramatic date of this dialogue (433/2 B.C.). However, Plato does not seem to have been afraid of anachronisms.]

[24] [Eurybatus and Phrynondas were proverbial types of the scum of the earth.]

more, as they themselves confess. And therefore I have intro-
duced the following mode of payment. When a man has been
my pupil, if he so desires he pays my price, and if he does
not, he has only to go into a temple and take an oath of the   c
value of the instruction, and he pays no more than he declares
to be their value.[25]

Such is my myth, Socrates, and such is the argument by
which I endeavor to show that virtue may be taught, and that
this is the opinion of the Athenians. And I have also attempted to show that you are not to wonder at good fathers
having bad sons, or at good sons having bad fathers. The sons
of Polycleitus,[26] who are the companions of our two friends
here, Paralus and Xanthippus, afford an example of this: they
are insignificant in comparison with their father; and this is
true of the sons of many other artists. As yet I ought not to
say the same of Paralus and Xanthippus themselves, for they   d
are young and there is still hope for them.

5. *Socrates and Protagoras: First Round* (328d–334c)

Protagoras finished his *tour de force* and came to the end
of his argument, and in my ear

So charming left his voice, that I the while
Thought him still speaking; still stood fixed to hear.[27]

At length, when the truth dawned upon me that he had really
finished, not without difficulty I began to collect myself; and
looking at Hippocrates, I said to him: O son of Apollodorus,
how deeply grateful I am to you for having brought me
hither; I would not have missed the speech of Protagoras for
a great deal. For I used to imagine that no human care could   e
make men good; but I know better now. Yet I have still one

---

25 [See Aulus Gellius (*Attic Nights*, V, 10) for an amusing variant.]

26 [Polycleitus, the famous sculptor of the second half of the fifth
century B.C., has been mentioned at 311c in this dialogue. Nothing is
known of his sons apart from the information given here.]

27 [Borrowed by Milton, *Paradise Lost*, VIII, 2-3.]

very small difficulty which I am sure that Protagoras will easily explain, as he has already explained so much. If a man were to go and consult Pericles or any of our great speakers about these matters, he might perhaps hear as fine a discourse; but then when one has a question to ask of any of them, like books, they can neither answer nor ask, and if anyone challenges the least particular of their speech, they go ringing on in a long harangue, like brazen pots, which when they are struck continue to sound unless someone puts his hand upon them. Whereas our friend Protagoras cannot only make a good long speech, as he has already shown, but when he is asked a question he can answer briefly; and when he asks he will wait and hear the answer. And this is a very rare gift. Now I, Protagoras, want to ask of you a little question, which if you will only answer, I shall be quite satisfied. You were saying that virtue can be taught—that I will take upon your authority, and there is no one to whom I am more ready to trust. But I marvel at one thing about which I should like to have my mind set at rest. You were speaking of Zeus sending justice and reverence to men, and several times while you were speaking, justice, and self-control, and piety, and all these qualities were described by you as if they could be lumped together into one thing, namely, virtue. Now I want you to tell me exactly whether virtue is one whole, of which justice and self-control and piety are parts; or whether all these are only the names of one and the same thing. That is the doubt which still lingers in my mind.

There is no difficulty, Socrates, in answering that the qualities of which you are speaking are the parts of virtue which is one.

And are they parts, I said, in the same sense in which mouth, nose, and eyes, and ears, are the parts of a face; or are they like the parts of gold, which differ from the whole and from one another only in being larger or smaller?

I should say that they differed, Socrates, in the first way; they are related to one another as the parts of a face are related to the whole face.

And do some men have one part and some another part of virtue? Or if a man has one part, must he also have all the others?

By no means, he said; for many a man is courageous and not just, or just and not wise.

You would not deny, then, I replied, that courage and 330 wisdom are also parts of virtue?

Most undoubtedly they are, he answered; and wisdom is the most important of the parts.

And they are all different from one another? I said.

Yes.

And has each of them a distinct function like the parts of the face? The eye, for example, is not like the ear and has not the same function; and of the other parts none is like another, either in their functions, or in any other way. I want to know whether the comparison holds concerning the parts of virtue. Do they also differ from one another in themselves and in their functions? For that is clearly what the simile b would imply.

Yes, Socrates, you are right in supposing that they differ.

Then, I said, no other part of virtue is like knowledge, or like justice, or like courage, or like self-control, or like piety?

No, he answered.

(a) The Unity of Justice and Piety (330c–332a)

Well then, I said, suppose that you and I inquire into the particular nature of each. And first, you would agree with me that justice is some particular thing, is it not? That is my c opinion; would it not be yours also?

Mine also, he said.

And suppose that someone were to ask us, saying "O, Protagoras, and you, Socrates, what about this thing which you were calling justice, is it just or unjust?" and I were to answer, just. How would you vote, with me or against me?

With you, he said.

Thereupon I should answer to him who asked me, that justice is of the nature of the just. Would not you?

Yes, he said.

And suppose that he went on to say: "Well now, is there also such a thing as piety?" we should answer "Yes," if I am not mistaken.

d   Yes, he said.

Which you would also acknowledge to be a thing—should we not say so?

He assented.

"And is this a sort of thing which is of the nature of the pious, or of the nature of the impious?" I should be angry at his putting such a question, and should say, "Peace, man, nothing can be pious if piety is not pious." What would you

e   say? Would you not answer in the same way?

Certainly, he said.

And then after this suppose that he came and asked us, "What were you saying just now? Perhaps I may not have heard you rightly, but you seemed to me to be saying that the parts of virtue in their mutual relation were not the same as one another." I should reply, "You certainly heard that said, but not, as you imagine, by me; for I only asked the

331   question; Protagoras gave the answer." And suppose that he turned to you and said, "Is this true, Protagoras? And do you maintain that one part of virtue is unlike another, and is this your position?" How would you answer him?

I could not help acknowledging the truth of what he said, Socrates.

Well then, Protagoras, we will assume this. And now supposing that he proceeded to say further, "Then piety is not of the nature of a just thing, nor justice of the nature of a pious thing, but of the nature of an impious thing; and piety of the nature of the not just, and therefore of the unjust, and

b   the unjust is the impious." How shall we answer him? I should certainly answer him on my own behalf that justice is pious, and that piety is just; and I would say in like manner on your behalf also, if you would allow me, that justice is either the same with piety, or very nearly the same; and above all I would assert that justice is like piety and piety is like justice. And I wish that you would tell me whether I may be permitted to give this answer on your behalf, and whether you would agree with me.

He replied: This matter does not seem to be quite so simple, Socrates, that I can agree to the proposition that justice is pious and that piety is just, for there appears to me to be a difference between them. But what matter? If you please I please; and let us assume, if you will, that justice is pious and that piety is just.   c

Pardon me, I replied. I do not want this "if you please" or "if you like" sort of proposition to be put to the test, but I want you and me to be tested. I mean to say that the proposition will be best tested, if you take the "if" out of it.   d

Well, he said, I admit that justice bears a resemblance to piety, for there is always some point of view in which everything is like every other thing; white is in a certain way like black, and hard is like soft, and the most extreme opposites have some qualities in common. Even the parts of the face which, as we were saying before, are distinct and have different functions are still in a certain point of view similar, and one of them is like another of them. And you may prove, if you please, on the same principle that all things are like one another. And yet things which are alike in some particular ought not to be called alike, nor things which are unlike in some particular, however slight, unlike.   e

And do you think, I said in a tone of surprise, that justice and piety have but a small degree of likeness?

Certainly not; any more than I agree with what I understand to be your view.   332

(b) The Unity of Wisdom and Self-Control (332a–333b)

Well, I said, as you appear to be unhappy about this, let us take another of the examples which you mentioned instead. Do you admit the existence of folly?

I do.

✓   And is not wisdom the very opposite of folly?

That is true, he said.

And when men act rightly and advantageously, do they seem to you to be self-controlled or not?

Yes, he said.

And self-control makes them self-controlled?

b   Certainly.

And they who do not act rightly act foolishly, and in acting thus are not self-controlled?

I agree, he said.

Then to act foolishly is the opposite of acting with self-control?

He assented.

And foolish actions are done by folly, and self-controlled actions by self-control?

He agreed.

And that is done strongly which is done by strength, and that which is weakly done, by weakness?

He assented.

c   And that which is done with swiftness is done swiftly, and that which is done with slowness, slowly?

He assented again.

And that which is done in the same way is done by the same; and that which is done in opposite ways, by opposites?

He agreed.

Once more, I said, is there anything beautiful?

Yes.

To which the only opposite is the ugly?

There is no other.

And is there anything good?

There is.

To which the only opposite is the evil?

There is no other.

And there is the high in tone?

True.

To which the only opposite is the low?

There is no other, he said, but that.

Then every opposite has one opposite only and no more?

He assented.

Then now, I said, let us recapitulate our admissions. First   d
of all, we admitted that everything has one opposite and not
more than one?

We did so.

And we admitted also that what was done in opposite
ways was done by opposites?

Yes.

And that which was done foolishly, as we further admitted, was done in the opposite way to that which was done
with self-control?

Yes.

And that which was done with self-control was done by
self-control, and that which was done foolishly by folly?

He agreed.

And that which is done in opposite ways is done by op-   e
posites?

Yes.

And one thing is done by self-control, and quite another
thing by folly?

Yes.

And in opposite ways?

Certainly.

And therefore by opposites?

Yes.

Then folly is the opposite of self-control?

Clearly.

And do you remember that folly has already been acknowledged by us to be the opposite of wisdom?

He assented.

And we said that everything has only one opposite?

Yes.

Then, Protagoras, which of the two assertions shall we   333
renounce? One says that everything has but one opposite; the
other that wisdom is distinct from self-control, and that both

of them are parts of virtue; and that they are not only distinct, but dissimilar, both in themselves and in their functions, like the parts of a face. Which of these two assertions
shall we renounce? For both of them together are certainly
not in harmony, they do not accord or agree; for how can
they be said to agree if everything can have only one opposite

b   and not more than one, and yet folly, which is one, has clearly
the two opposites—wisdom and self-control. Is not that true,
Protagoras? What else would you say?

He assented, but with great reluctance.

Then self-control and wisdom are the same, as before
justice and piety appeared to us to be nearly the same. And

(c) The Unity of Self-Control and Justice (333b–334c)

now, Protagoras, I said, we must finish the inquiry, and not
give up. Do you think that an unjust man can be self-con-

c   trolled in his injustice?

I should be ashamed, Socrates, he said, to acknowledge
this which nevertheless many may be found to assert.

And shall I argue with them or with you? I replied.

I would rather, he said, that you should argue with the
many first, if you will.

It makes no difference to me, if you will only answer me
and say whether you are of their opinion or not. My object
is to test the validity of the argument, and yet the result may
be that I who ask and you who answer will both be tested.

d   Protagoras at first played coy and said that the argument
was not encouraging; at length he consented to answer.

Now then, I said, begin at the beginning and answer me.
You think that some men are self-controlled, and yet unjust?

Yes, he said, let that be admitted.

And self-control is good sense?

Yes.

And good sense is good counsel in doing injustice?

Granted.

If they do well, I said, or if they do not do well?

If they do well.

And you would admit the existence of goods?

Yes.

And is the good that which is advantageous for man?

Yes, indeed, he said: and there are some things which   e
may not be advantageous, and yet I call them good.

I thought that Protagoras was getting ruffled and excited;
he seemed to be marshaling his powers for a retort. Seeing
this, I minded my business, and gently said:

When you say, Protagoras, that things not advantageous
are good, do you mean not advantageous for man only, or   334
not advantageous altogether? And do you call the latter good?

Certainly not the last, he replied, for I know of many
things—meats, drinks, medicines, and ten thousand other
things which are not advantageous for man, and some which
are advantageous; and some which are neither advantageous
nor disadvantageous for man, but only for horses; and some
for oxen only and some for dogs; and some for no animals
but only for trees, and some for the roots of trees and not
for their branches, as for example manure, which is a good
thing when laid about the roots of any plant, but utterly de-   b
structive if thrown upon the shoots and young branches. Or I
may instance olive oil, which is mischievous to all plants, and
generally most injurious to the hair of every animal with the
exception of man, but beneficial to human hair and to the
human body generally. And even in this application (so various and changeable is the nature of the benefit) that which is
the greatest good to the exterior of the human body is a very   c
great evil to its interior, and for this reason physicians always
forbid their patients the use of oil in their food, except in
very small quantities, just enough to extinguish the disagree-
able sensation of smell in meats and sauces.

6. *Interlude* (334c–338e)

When he had given this answer, the company cheered him. And I said: Protagoras, I have a wretched memory, and when anyone makes a long speech to me I never remember
d   what he is talking about. As then, if I had been deaf and you were going to converse with me, you would have had to raise your voice, so now, having such a bad memory, I will ask you to cut your answers shorter, if you would take me with you.

What do you mean? he said. How am I to shorten my answers? Shall I make them too short?

Certainly not, I said.

But short enough?

e   Yes, I said.

Shall I answer what appears to me to be short enough, or what appears to you to be short enough?

I have heard, I said, that you can speak and teach others to speak about the same things at such length that words
335   never seemed to fail, or with such brevity that no one could use fewer of them. Please therefore, if you talk with me, to adopt the latter or more compendious method.

Socrates, he replied, many a battle of words have I fought, and if I had followed the method of disputation which my adversaries desired, as you want me to do, I should have been no better than another, and the name of Protagoras would not have spread all over Hellas.

I saw that he was not satisfied with his previous answers,
b   and that he would not play the part of answerer any more if he could help; and I considered that there was no call upon me to continue the conversation. So I said: Protagoras, I do not wish to force the conversation upon you if you had rather not, but when you are willing to argue with me in such a way that I can follow you, then I will argue with you. Now you, as is said of you by others and as you say of yourself, are able to have discussions in shorter forms of speech as well as

in longer, for you are a master of wisdom; but I cannot manage these long speeches. I only wish that I could. You, on the other hand, who are capable of either, ought to speak shorter as I beg you, and then we might converse. But I see that you are disinclined, and as I have an engagement which will prevent my staying to hear you at greater length (for I have to be in another place), I will depart, although I should have liked to have heard you.

Thus I spoke and was rising from my seat with the intention of leaving when Callias seized me by the right hand, and in his left hand caught hold of this old cloak of mine. He said: We shall not let you go, Socrates, for if you leave us this will be the end of our discussion. I must therefore beg you to remain, as there is nothing in the world that I should like better than to hear you and Protagoras discourse. Do not deny the company this pleasure.

Now I had got up, and was on the verge of departing. Son of Hipponicus, I replied, I have always admired and do now heartily applaud and love your desire for wisdom, and would gladly comply with your request if I could. But the truth is that I cannot. And what you ask is as great an impossibility to me as if you bade me run a race and keep pace with Crison of Himera[28] when in his prime, or with some long-distance runner or courier. To such a request I should reply that I would fain ask the same of my own legs, but they refuse to comply. And therefore, if you want to see Crison and me in the same race, you must bid him slacken his speed to mine, for I cannot run quickly, and he can run slowly. And in like manner, if you want to hear me and Protagoras discoursing, you must ask him to shorten his answers and keep to the point, as he did at first; if not, how can there be any discussion? For discussion is one thing, and making an oration is quite another, in my humble opinion.

28 [Crison of Himera was one of the most outstanding contemporary athletes. He had won footraces at the Olympic Games in 448, 444, and 440 B.C.]

But you see, Socrates, said Callias, that Protagoras may fairly claim to speak in his own way, just as you claim to speak in yours.

Here Alcibiades interposed, and said: That, Callias, is not a true statement of the case. For our friend Socrates admits that he cannot make a speech—in this he yields the palm to Protagoras; but I should be greatly surprised if he yielded

c to any living man in the ability to handle the give and take of argument. Now if Protagoras will make a similar admission, and confess that he is inferior to Socrates in argumentative skill, that is enough for Socrates. But if he claims a superiority in argument as well, let him ask and answer—not, when a question is asked, slipping away from the point and, instead of answering, making a speech at such length that

d most of his hearers forget the question at issue (not that Socrates is likely to forget, I will be bound for that, although he may pretend in fun that he has a bad memory). And Socrates appears to me to be more in the right than Protagoras. That is my view, and every man ought to say what he thinks.

When Alcibiades had done speaking, someone—Critias, I believe—spoke: O Prodicus and Hippias, Callias appears to

e me to be a partisan of Protagoras. And this led Alcibiades, who loves opposition, to take the other side. But we should not be partisans either of Socrates or of Protagoras. Let us rather unite in entreating both of them not to break up the discussion.

337 Prodicus added: That, Critias, seems to me to be well said, for those who are present at such discussions ought to be impartial hearers of both the speakers, remembering, however, that impartiality is not the same as equality, for both sides should be impartially heard, and yet an equal need should not be assigned to both of them, but to the wiser a higher need should be given, and a lower to the less wise. And I as well as Critias would beg you, Protagoras and Socrates, to

b grant our request which is that you will dispute with one another and not wrangle, for friends dispute with friends out of good will, but only adversaries and enemies wrangle. And

then our meeting will be most delightful, for in this way you, who are the speakers, will be most likely to win esteem, and not praise only, among us who are your audience. For esteem is a sincere conviction of the hearers' souls, but praise is often an insincere, verbal expression of men uttering falsehoods contrary to their conviction. And thus we, who are the hearers, will be gratified and not pleased, for gratification is of the   c
mind when receiving wisdom and knowledge, but pleasure is of the body when eating or experiencing some other bodily delight. Thus spoke Prodicus, and many of the company applauded his words.

Hippias the sage spoke next. He said: All of you who are here present I reckon to be kinsmen and friends and fellow citizens by nature and not by convention, for by nature like   d
is akin to like, whereas convention is the tyrant of mankind and often compels us to do many things which are against nature. How great would be the disgrace then if we, who know the nature of things and are the wisest of the Hellenes, and as such are met together in this city, which is the center of wisdom in Hellas, and in the greatest and most glorious house of this city, should have nothing to show worthy of this height of dignity, but should only quarrel with one another   e
like the meanest of mankind! I do pray and advise you, Protagoras, and you, Socrates, to agree upon a compromise. Let us be your peacemakers. And do not you, Socrates, aim at this   338
precise and extreme brevity in discourse, if Protagoras objects, but loosen and let go the reins of speech, that your words may present themselves grander and more graceful before us. Neither do you, Protagoras, go forth on the gale with every sail set out of sight of land into an ocean of words, but let there be a mean observed by both of you. Do as I say. And let me also persuade you to choose an umpire or overseer or president; he will keep watch over your words and will prescribe   b
their proper length.

This proposal was received by the company with universal approval. Callias said that he would not let me off, and they begged me to choose an overseer. But I said that to

choose an umpire of discourse would be unseemly, for if the
person chosen was inferior, then the inferior or worse ought
not to preside over the better; or if he was equal, neither
would that be well, for he who is our equal will do as we do,
and what will be the use of choosing him? And if you say,
c "Let us have a better, then," to that I answer that, as a matter
of fact, you cannot have anyone who is wiser than Protagoras.
And if you choose another who is not really better, and who
you only say is better, to put another over him as though he
were an inferior person would be an unworthy reflection on
him—not that, as far as I am concerned, any reflection is of
much consequence to me. Let me tell you then what I will
do in order that the conversation and discussion may go on
d as you desire. If Protagoras is not disposed to answer, let him
ask and I will answer, and I will endeavor to show at the
same time how, as I maintain, he ought to answer; and when
I have answered as many questions as he likes to ask, let him
in like manner answer me. And if he seems to be not very
ready at answering the precise question asked of him, you and
I will unite in entreating him, as you entreated me, not to
e spoil the discussion. And this will require no special overseer
—all of you shall be overseers together.

This was generally approved, and Protagoras, though very
much against his will, was obliged to agree that he would ask
questions; and when he had put a sufficient number of them,
that he would answer in his turn those which he was asked
in short replies. He began to put his questions as follows:

Criticism

7. Socrates Interprets a Poet (338e–348a)

I am of opinion, Socrates, he said, that skill in poetry is
the principal part of education; and this I conceive to be the
339 ability to understand which compositions of the poets are
correct, and which are not, and to know how to distinguish
between them and, when asked, give the reasons. And I propose to transfer the question which you and I have been discussing to the domain of poetry; we will speak as before of

virtue, but in reference to a passage of a poet. Now Simonides says to Scopas, the son of Creon the Thessalian:

It is with difficulty that, on the one hand, a man can become **b** truly good, built foursquare in hands and feet and mind, a work without a flaw.[29]

Do you know the poem? Or shall I repeat the whole?

There is no need, I said; for I am perfectly well acquainted with the ode—I have made a careful study of it.

Very well, he said. And do you think that the ode is a good composition, and true?

Yes, I said, both good and true.

But if there is a contradiction, can the composition be good or true?

No, not in that case, I replied.

And is there not a contradiction? he asked. Reflect.

Well, my friend, I have reflected. **c**

And does not the poet proceed to say, "I do not agree with the word of Pittacus,[30] albeit the utterance of a wise man: 'With difficulty can a man be good' "? Now you will observe that this is said by the same poet who made the first statement.

I know it.

And do you think, he said, that the two sayings are consistent?

Yes, I said, I think so (at the same time I could not help fearing that there might be something in what he said). And you think otherwise?

Why, he said, how can he be consistent in both? First of **d** all, premising as his own thought, "It is with difficulty that

29 [Simonides of Ceos (*ca.* 556-468 B.C.) was a lyric and elegiac poet. He is perhaps best known for his epigrams celebrating the victories over the Persians at Marathon and Thermopylae. The poem discussed here was perhaps a drinking song written during Simonides' stay with the Scopads in Thessaly in the last decade of the sixth century B.C.]

30 [Pittacus (*ca.* 650-570 B.C.) was a great statesman and reformer in Mytilene on the island of Lesbos. He was counted among the Seven Wise Men in ancient tradition.]

a man can become truly good," and then a little further on in the poem, forgetting, and blaming Pittacus and refusing to agree with him, when he says, "With difficulty can a man be good," which is the very same thing. And yet when he blames him who says the same with himself, he obviously also blames himself, so that he must be wrong either in his first or his second assertion.

Many of the audience cheered and applauded this. And I felt at first giddy and faint, as if I had received a blow from the hand of an expert boxer, when I heard his words and the sound of the cheering; and to tell you the truth, I wanted to get time to think what the meaning of the poet really was. So I turned to Prodicus and called him. Prodicus, I said, Simonides is a countryman of yours, and you ought to come to his aid. I must appeal to you, like the river Scamander in Homer who, when beleaguered by Achilles, summons the Simoïs to aid him, saying: "Brother dear, let us both together stay the force of the hero." [31] And I summon you, for I am afraid that Protagoras will make an end of Simonides. Now is the time to rehabilitate Simonides by the application of your literary art which enables you to distinguish "will" and "wish," and make other charming distinctions like those which you drew just now. And I should like to know whether you would agree with me, for I am of opinion that there is no contradiction in the words of Simonides. And first of all I wish that you would say whether, in your opinion, Prodicus, "being" is the same as "becoming."

Not the same, certainly, replied Prodicus.

Did not Simonides first set forth, as his own view, that it would be with difficulty that a man can *become* truly good?

Quite right, said Prodicus.

And then he blames Pittacus, not, as Protagoras imagines, for repeating that which he says himself, but for saying something different from himself. Pittacus does not say, as Simonides says, that with difficulty can a man become good, but with difficulty can a man *be* good. And our friend Prodicus

[31] *Iliad*, XXI, 308.

would maintain that being, Protagoras, is not the same as becoming; and if they are not the same, then Simonides is not inconsistent with himself. I dare say that Prodicus and many others would say, as Hesiod says,

On the one hand, 'tis difficult for a man to become good,
For the gods have made virtue the reward of toil;
But on the other hand, when you have climbed the height,
Then, to retain virtue, however difficult the acquisition, is
    easy.[32]

Prodicus heard and approved, but Protagoras said: Your rehabilitation, Socrates, involves a greater error than is contained in the sentence which you are correcting.

Alas! I said, Protagoras, then I am a sorry physician, and do but aggravate a disorder which I am seeking to cure.

Such is the fact, he said.

How so? I asked.

It would reflect great ignorance on the part of the poet, he replied, if he says that virtue, which in the opinion of all men is the hardest of all things, can be easily retained.

Well, I said, and how fortunate are we in having Prodicus among us, at the right moment, for he has a wisdom, Protagoras, which as I imagine is more than human and of very ancient date, and may be as old as Simonides or even older. Learned as you are in many things, you appear to know nothing of this. But I know, for I am a disciple of Prodicus here. And now, if I am not mistaken, you do not understand the word "difficult" (χαλεπόν) in the sense which Simonides intended; and I must correct you, as Prodicus corrects me when I use the word "awful" (δεινόν) as a term of praise. If I say that Protagoras or anyone else is an "awfully" wise man, he asks me if I am not ashamed of calling that which is good "awful"; and then he explains to me that the term "awful" is always taken in a bad sense, and that no one speaks of being "awfully" healthy or wealthy, or "awful" peace, but of "awful" disease, "awful" war, "awful" poverty, meaning by the term

---

[32] *Works and Days*, 264f.

"awful" evil. And I think that Simonides and his country-men the Ceans, when they spoke of "difficult," meant "evil," or something which you do not understand. Let us ask Prodi-cus, for he ought to be able to answer questions about the dialect of Simonides. What did he mean, Prodicus, by the term "difficult"?

c

Evil, said Prodicus.

And therefore, I said, Prodicus, he blames Pittacus for saying, "It is difficult to be good," just as if that were equiva-lent to saying, "It is evil to be good."

Yes, he said, that was certainly his meaning; and he is twitting Pittacus with ignorance of the use of terms, which in a Lesbian, who has been accustomed to speak a barbarous language, is natural.

Do you hear, Protagoras, I asked, what our friend Prodi-cus is saying? And have you an answer for him?

d

You are entirely mistaken, Prodicus, said Protagoras, and I know very well that Simonides in using the word "difficult" meant what all of us mean, not evil, but that which is not easy—that which takes a great deal of trouble.

I said: I also incline to believe, Protagoras, that this was the meaning of Simonides, of which our friend Prodicus was very well aware, but he thought that he would make fun and see if you could maintain your thesis. For that Simonides could never have meant the other is clearly proved by the context, in which he says that god only has this gift. Now he cannot surely mean to say that to be good is evil, when he afterwards proceeds to say that a god only has this gift, and that this is the attribute of him and of no other. For if this be his meaning, Prodicus would impute to Simonides a char-acter of recklessness which is very unlike his countrymen. And I should like to tell you, I said, what I imagine to be the real meaning of Simonides in this poem, if you will test what, in your way of speaking, would be called my skill in poetry; or if you would rather, I will be the listener.

e

342

To this proposal Protagoras replied: As you please. And

Hippias, Prodicus, and the others told me by all means to do as I proposed.

Then now, I said, I will endeavor to explain to you my opinion about this poem of Simonides. There is a very ancient philosophy which is more cultivated in Crete and Lacedaemon than in any other part of Hellas, and there are more philosophers in those countries than anywhere else in the world. This, however, is a secret which these people deny; and they pretend to be ignorant, just because they do not wish to have it thought that they excel the other Hellenes by reason of their wisdom, like the Sophists of whom Protagoras was speaking, but that they surpass the rest by reason of their fighting ability and their courage, considering that if the reason of their superiority were disclosed, all men would be practicing their wisdom. And this secret of theirs has never been discovered by the imitators of Lacedaemonian fashions in other cities, who go about with their ears bruised in imitation of them, and have the caestus [gloves] of boxers bound on their arms, and are always in training, and wear short cloaks; for they imagine that these are the practices which have enabled the Lacedaemonians to conquer the other Hellenes. Now when the Lacedaemonians want to unbend and hold free conversation with their wise men, and are no longer satisfied with mere secret intercourse, they drive out all these laconizers, and any other foreigners who may happen to be in their country, and they hold a philosophical *séance* unknown to strangers; and they themselves forbid their young men to go out into other cities—in this they are like the Cretans—in order that they may not unlearn the lessons which they have taught them. And in Lacedaemon and Crete not only men but also women have a pride in their high level of education. And hereby you may know that I am right in attributing to the Lacedaemonians this excellence in philosophy and discourse: if a man converses with the most ordinary Lacedaemonian, he will find him seldom good for much in general conversation, but at a point in the discourse he will inject some notable saying, short and terse, with unerring aim, like a sharpshooter; and the person with whom he is talking seems to be like a child in his hands. And many of our own age and of former ages have noted that the true Lacedaemonian type of character has the love of wisdom even stronger than the love of physical exercise. They are conscious that only a perfectly educated man is capable of uttering such expressions. Such were Thales of Miletus, and Pittacus of Mytilene, and Bias of Priene, and our own Solon, and Cleobulus of Lindus, and Myson of Chenae [33]; and seventh in the catalogue of wise men was the Lacedaemonian Chilo. All these were lovers and emulators and disciples of the culture of the Lacedaemonians, and anyone may perceive that their wisdom was of this character, consisting of short memorable sentences, which they severally uttered. And they met together and dedicated in the temple of Apollo at Delphi, as the first fruits of their wisdom, the far-famed inscriptions which are in all men's mouths, "Know thyself," and "Nothing in excess."

Why do I say all this? I am explaining that this Lacedaemonian brevity was the style of ancient philosophy. Now there was a saying of Pittacus which was privately circulated and received the approbation of the wise, "Difficult is it to be good." And Simonides, who was ambitious of the fame of wisdom, was aware that if he could overthrow this saying, then, as if he had won a victory over some famous athlete, he would carry off the palm among his contemporaries. And if I am not mistaken, he composed the entire poem with the secret intention of damaging Pittacus and his saying.

Let us all unite in examining his poem and see whether I am speaking the truth. Simonides must have been a lunatic if, in the very first words of the poem, wanting to say only that to become good is hard, he inserted μέν, "on the one hand" ("on the one hand to become good is difficult"); there would be no reason for the introduction of μέν unless you suppose

[33] [In the list of the Seven Wise Men given by Plutarch in his *Banquet of the Seven Wise Men*, Periander, the tyrant of Corinth, takes the place of Myson.]

Simonides to speak with a hostile reference to the words of
Pittacus. Pittacus is saying, "Difficult is it to be good," and
he, in refutation of this thesis, rejoins that the truly difficult
thing, Pittacus, is to become good, not joining "truly" with
"good," but with "difficult." Not that the hard thing is to be
truly good, as though there were some truly good men, and
there were others who were good but not truly good (this
would be a very naïve observation, and quite unworthy of
Simonides); but you must suppose him to make a poetic tra-
jection of the word "truly" (ἀλαθέως), construing the saying
of Pittacus thus (and let us imagine Pittacus to be speaking
and Simonides answering him): "O my friends," says Pittacus,
"difficult is it to be good," and Simonides answers: "In that,
Pittacus, you are mistaken; the difficulty is not to be good
but, on the one hand, to become good, foursquare in hands
and feet and mind, wrought without a flaw—that is difficult
truly." This way of reading the passage accounts for the in-
sertion of μέν, "on the one hand," and for the position at the
end of the clause of the word "truly," and all that follows
shows this to be the meaning. A great deal might be said to
demonstrate the excellent composition of each detail of the
poem, which is a charming piece of workmanship, and very
finished, but such minutiae would be tedious. I should like,
however, to point out the general outline and intention of
the poem, which is certainly designed in every part to be a
refutation of the saying of Pittacus.

For he speaks in what follows a little further on as if he
meant to argue prosaically that although there truly is a
difficulty in becoming good, yet this is possible for a time, and
only for a time. But having become good, to remain in a
good state and be good, as you, Pittacus, affirm, is not possible, and is not granted to man; a god only has this blessing,
"but man cannot help being bad when the force of circumstances overpowers him." Now whom does the force of circumstances overpower in the command of a vessel? Not the
layman, for he is always overpowered. And as one who is
already prostrate cannot be overthrown, and only he who is

e

344

b

c

standing upright, but not he who is prostrate, can be laid prostrate, so the force of circumstances can only overpower him who at some time or other has resources, and not him who is at all times helpless. The descent of a great storm may make the pilot helpless, or the severity of the season the farmer or the physician. For the good may become bad, as another poet witnesses: "The good are sometimes good and sometimes bad." [34] But the bad does not become bad; he is necessarily always bad. So that when the force of circumstances overpowers the man of resources and wisdom and virtue, then he cannot help being bad. And you, Pittacus, are saying, "Difficult is it to be good." Now there is a difficulty in becoming good, and yet this is possible. But to be good is an impossibility—"For he who does well is the good man, and he who does ill is the bad." But what constitutes "doing well" in writing? And what kind of activity makes a man good in writing? Clearly, learning it. And what sort of well-doing makes a man a good physician? Clearly, learning the art of healing the sick. "But he who does ill is the bad." Now who becomes a bad physician? Clearly, he who is in the first place a physician, and in the second place a good physician; for he may become a bad one also. But none of us unskilled individuals can by any amount of doing ill become physicians, any more than we can become carpenters or anything of that sort. And he who by doing ill cannot become a physician at all clearly cannot become a bad physician. In like manner the good may become bad by time, or toil, or disease, or other accident (the only real doing ill is to be deprived of knowledge), but the bad man will never become bad, for he is always bad, and if he were to become bad, he must previously have been good. Thus the words of the poem tend to show that on the one hand a man cannot be continuously good, but that he may become good and may also become bad. And again that "They are the best for the longest time whom the gods love."

[34] [The authorship of this passage, which is also quoted by Socrates in Xenophon's *Memorabilia*, I, ii, 20, is not known.]

All this relates to Pittacus, as the sequel makes even clearer. For he adds:

Therefore I will not throw away my span of life to no purpose in searching after the impossible, hoping in vain to find a perfectly faultless man among those who partake of the fruit of the broad-bosomed earth: if I find him, I will send you word.

(This is the vehement way in which he pursues his attack upon Pittacus throughout the whole poem):

But him who does no evil, voluntarily I praise and love— not even the gods war against necessity.

All this has a similar drift, for Simonides was not so ignorant as to say that he praised those who did no evil voluntarily as though there were some who did evil voluntarily. For no wise man, as I believe, will allow that any human being errs voluntarily, or voluntarily does evil and base actions; but they are very well aware that all who do evil and base things do them against their will. And Simonides never says that he praises him who does no evil voluntarily; the word "voluntarily" applies to himself. For he was under the impression that a good man might often force himself to become the friend and approver of another; and that there might be an enforced love, such as a man might feel to an unnatural father or mother, or country, or the like. Now bad men, when their parents or country have any defects, look on them with malignant joy, and find fault with them and expose and denounce them to others, under the idea that the rest of mankind will be less likely to take themselves to task and accuse them of neglect; and they blame their defects far more than they deserve, in order that the odium which is necessarily incurred by them may be increased. But the good man dissembles his feelings, and constrains himself to praise them; and if they have wronged him and he is angry, he pacifies his anger and is reconciled, and compels himself to love and praise his own flesh and blood. And Simonides, as is probable, considered that he himself had often had to praise and mag-

d

e

346

b

nify a tyrant or the like, not of his own free will, but by such
constraint, and he also wishes to imply to Pittacus that he
c   does not censure him because he is censorious.

For I am satisfied (he says) when a man is neither bad nor
excessively foolish, and when he knows justice (which is the
health of states), and is of sound mind, I will find no fault
with him, for I am not given to finding fault, and there are
innumerable fools

(implying that if someone delights in censure he has abundant
opportunity of finding fault).

"All things are good with which evil is unmingled." In
d   these latter words he does not mean to say that all things are
good which have no evil in them, as you might say, "All things
are white which have no black in them," for that would be
ridiculous; but he means to say that he accepts and finds no
fault with the moderate or intermediate state.—

I do not hope (he says) to find a perfectly blameless man
among those who partake of the fruits of the broad-bosomed
earth (if I find him, I will send you word); in this sense I
praise no man. But he who is moderately good, and does no
evil, is good enough for me who love and approve everyone

e   (and here observe that he uses a Lesbian word, ἐπαίνημι (approve), because he is addressing Pittacus—

"I love and *approve* everyone *voluntarily,* who does no evil":

and that the stop should be put after "voluntarily"); "but
there are some whom I involuntarily praise and love. And
347   you, Pittacus, I would never have blamed if you had spoken
what was moderately good and true; but I do blame you because, putting on the appearance of truth, you are speaking
inordinately falsely about the highest matters." And this, I
said, Prodicus and Protagoras, I take to be the meaning of
Simonides in this poem.

Hippias said: I think, Socrates, that you have given a
very good explanation of the poem, but I have also an excel-

lent interpretation of my own which I will propound to you,   b
if you so desire.

Nay, Hippias, said Alcibiades, not now, but at some other
time. At present we must abide by the compact which was
made between Socrates and Protagoras, to the effect that as
long as Protagoras is willing to ask, Socrates should answer;
or that if he would rather answer, then that Socrates should
ask.

I said: I wish Protagoras either to ask or answer as he is
inclined. But I would rather have done with poems and odes,
if he does not object, and come back to the question about
which I was asking you at first, Protagoras, and by your help   c
make an end of that investigation. The talk about poetry
seems to me like a commonplace entertainment at the ban-
quets of the vulgar who, because they are not able to converse
with or amuse one another while they are drinking, with the
sound of their own voices and conversation, by reason of their
stupidity, raise the price of flute-girls, hiring for a great sum   d
the voice of a flute instead of their own breath, to be the
medium of intercourse among them. But where the company
are real gentlemen and men of education, you will see no
flute-girls, nor dancing girls, nor harp-girls, and they have no
nonsense or games, but are contented with one another's conversation, of which their own voices are the medium and
which they carry on by turns and in an orderly manner, even
though they consume a lot of wine. And a company like this   e
of ours, and men such as we profess to be, do not require the
help of another's voice, or of the poets whom you cannot
interrogate about the meaning of what they are saying; people
who cite them declaring, some that the poet has one meaning,
and others that he has another, and the point which is in
dispute can never be decided. This sort of entertainment they
decline and prefer to talk with one another, and put one an-   348
other to the proof in conversation. And these are the models
which I desire that you and I should imitate. Leaving the
poets and keeping to ourselves, let us try the mettle of one

another and make proof of the truth in conversation. If you have a mind to ask, I am ready to answer; or if you would rather, do you answer, and give me the opportunity of resuming and completing our unfinished argument.

8. *Socrates and Protagoras: Second Round* (348b–360e)

b   I made these and some similar observations; but Protagoras would not distinctly say which he would do. Thereupon Alcibiades turned to Callias and said: Do you think, Callias, that Protagoras is fair in refusing to say whether he will or will not answer? For I certainly think that he is unfair. He ought either to proceed with the argument or distinctly to refuse to proceed, that we may know his intention; and then Socrates will be able to discourse with someone else, and the rest of the company will be free to talk with one another.

c   I think that Protagoras was really made ashamed by these words of Alcibiades, and when the prayers of Callias and some of the others were superadded, he was at last induced to argue, and said that I might ask and he would answer.

So I said: Do not imagine, Protagoras, that I have any other interest in asking questions of you but that of clearing up my own problems as they arise. For I think that Homer

d   was very right in saying that "When two go together, one sees before the other," [35] for all men who have a companion are readier in deed, word, or thought; but if a man "sees a thing when he is alone," he goes about straightway seeking until he finds someone to whom he may show his discoveries, and who may confirm him in them. And I would rather hold discourse with you than with anyone, because I think that no man can better investigate most things which a good man

e   may be expected to investigate, and in particular virtue. For who is there, but you?—who not only claim to be a good man and a gentleman, for many are this, and yet have not the power of making others good—whereas you are not only good

[35] *Iliad*, X, 224.

yourself, but also able to make others good. Moreover such
confidence have you in yourself that, although other Sophists
conceal their profession, you proclaim openly in the face of   349
all Hellas that you are a Sophist or teacher of virtue and education, and are the first who demanded pay in return. How
then can I do otherwise than invite you to the investigation
of these subjects, and ask questions and consult with you? I
must, indeed. And I should like once more to have my memory refreshed by you about the questions which I was asking
you at first, and also to have your help in considering them.
If I am not mistaken, the question was this: Are wisdom and   b
self-control and courage and justice and piety five names
which denote the same thing? Or is there, corresponding to
each of these names, a separate underlying reality, a thing
with its own peculiar function, no one of them being like any
other of them? And you replied that the five names did not
denote a single thing, but that each of them denoted a sepa-   c
rate thing, and that all of these things were parts of virtue,
not in the same way that the parts of gold are like each other
and like the whole of which they are parts, but as the parts
of the face are unlike the whole of which they are parts and
one another, and have each of them a distinct function. I
should like to know whether this is still your opinion; or if
not, I will ask you to define your meaning, and I shall not
take you to task if you now make a different statement. For
I dare say that you may have said what you did only in order
to make trial of me.   d

(a) The Unity of Courage and Wisdom (349d–351b)

I answer, Socrates, he said, that all these qualities are
parts of virtue, and that four out of the five are to some extent
similar, and that the fifth of them, which is courage, is very
different from the other four, as I prove in this way: You
may observe that many men are utterly unrighteous, impious,
self-indulgent, ignorant, who are nevertheless remarkable for
their courage.

e   Stop, I said; I should like to investigate that. When you speak of courageous men, do you mean the confident, or something else?

Yes, he said; I mean the aggressive, ready to go at that which most people are afraid to approach.

In the next place, you would affirm virtue to be a good thing, of which good thing you assert yourself to be a teacher?

Yes, he said; I should say the best of all things, if I am in my right mind.

And is it partly good and partly bad, I said, or wholly good?

Wholly good, and in the highest degree.

Tell me, then, who are they who have confidence when
350   diving into a well.

I should say, the divers.

And the reason of this is that they have knowledge?

Yes, that is the reason.

And who have confidence when fighting on horseback—the skilled horseman or the unskilled?

The skilled.

And who when fighting with light shields—the peltasts [36] or the nonpeltasts?

The peltasts. And that is true of all other cases, he said, if that is your point. Those who have knowledge are more confident than those who have no knowledge, and they are more confident after they have learned than before.

b   And have you not seen persons utterly ignorant, I said, of these things, and yet confident about them?

Yes, he said, I have seen such persons far too confident.

And are not these confident persons also courageous?

In that case, he replied, courage would be a base thing, for the men of whom we are speaking are surely madmen.

Then what do you mean when you speak of the courageous? Do you not mean that they are confident?

Yes, he said; to that statement I adhere.

[36] [Light-armed foot soldiers.]

And those, I said, who are thus confident without knowl-   c
edge are really not courageous, but mad. And in the former
case, on the other hand, those who are the wisest are also
most confident, and being most confident are most courageous.
According to this argument also wisdom would be courage.

Nay, Socrates, he replied, you are mistaken in your re-
membrance of what I said and answered to you. When you
asked me, I certainly did say that the courageous are the
confident; but I was never asked whether the confident are
the courageous. If you had asked me, I should have answered,
"Not all of them"; and what I did answer, namely, that the   d
courageous are confident, you have not proved to be false. Next
you proceeded to show that those who have knowledge are
more confident than they were before they had knowledge,
and more confident than others who have no knowledge, and
were then led on to think that courage is the same as wisdom.
But in this way of arguing you might come to imagine that
strength is wisdom. You might begin by asking whether the
strong are able, and I should say "Yes"; and then whether   e
those who know how to wrestle are not more able to wrestle
than those who do not know how to wrestle, and more able
after than before they had learned, and I should assent. And
when I had admitted this, you might use my admissions in
such a way as to prove that upon my view wisdom is strength;
whereas in that case I should not have admitted, any more
than in the other, that the able are strong, although I have
admitted that the strong are able. For there is a difference
between ability and strength. The former is given by knowl-   351
edge as well as by madness or rage, but strength comes from
nature and a healthy state of the body. And in like manner
I say of confidence and courage that they are not the same;
and I argue that the courageous are confident, but not all the
confident courageous. For confidence may be given to men by
art, and also, like ability, by madness and rage, but courage   b
comes to them from the nature and good nurture of the soul.

(b) The Power of Knowledge (351b–358d)

I said: You would admit, Protagoras, that some men live well and others ill?

He assented.

And do you think that a man lives well who lives in pain and grief?

He does not.

But if he lives pleasantly to the end of his life, will he not in that case have lived well?

He will.

c   Then to live pleasantly is good, and to live unpleasantly evil?

Yes, he said, if he lives so as to find pleasure in what is good and noble.

And do you, Protagoras, like the rest of the world, call some pleasant things evil and some painful things good? For I say that things are good in so far as they are pleasant if they have no consequences of another sort, and in so far as they are painful they are bad.

I do not know, Socrates, he said, whether I can venture to

d   assert in that unqualified manner in which you ask, that all pleasant things are good and the painful evil. Having regard not only to my present answer, but also to the whole of my life, I shall be safer, if I am not mistaken, in saying that there are some pleasant things which are not good, and that there are some painful things which are not evil, and some which are, and that there are some which are neither good nor evil.

And you would call pleasant, I said, the things which

e   participate in pleasure or create pleasure?

Certainly, he said.

Then my meaning is that in so far as they are pleasant they are good; and my question would imply that pleasure in itself is good.

According to your favorite mode of speech, Socrates, "let us investigate this," he said; and if the investigation is to the point, and the result proves that pleasure and good are really the same, then we will agree; but if not, then we will argue.

And would you wish to begin the inquiry, I said, or shall I begin?

You ought to take the lead, he said; for you are the author of the discussion.

May I employ an illustration? I said. Suppose someone   352
who is inquiring into the health or some other bodily function of another on the basis of that person's general appearance—he looks at his face and at the tips of his fingers, and then he says: Uncover your chest and back to me, that I may have a better view. That is the sort of thing that I desire in this investigation. Having seen what your attitude is toward good and pleasure, I am minded to say to you: Uncover your mind to me, Protagoras, and reveal your attitude toward   b
knowledge, that I may know whether or not you agree with the rest of the world. Now the rest of the world are of opinion that knowledge is not a powerful, lordly, commanding thing; they do not think of it as actually being anything of that sort at all, but their notion is that a man may have knowledge, and yet that the knowledge which is in him may be overmastered by anger, or pleasure, or pain, or love, or perhaps by fear—just as if knowledge were nothing but a slave and might   c
be dragged about by all these other things. Now is that your view? Or do you think that knowledge is a noble thing and fit to command in man, which cannot be overcome and will not allow a man, if he only knows the good and the evil, to do anything which is contrary to what his knowledge bids him do, but that wisdom will have strength to help him?

I agree with you, Socrates, said Protagoras; and not only so, but I, above all other men, am bound to say that wisdom   d
and knowledge are the mightiest of human things.

Good, I said, and true. But are you aware that the majority of the world do not share your conviction and mine, but claim that many people know the things which are best, but do not do them when they might? And most persons whom I

have asked the reason of this have said that when men act
contrary to knowledge they are overcome by pain, or pleasure,
or some of those things which I was just now mentioning.

Yes, Socrates, he replied; and that is not the only point
about which mankind is in error.

Suppose, then, that you and I endeavor to persuade and
explain to them what is the nature of this event which they
call "being overcome by pleasure," and which they affirm to
be the reason why they do not always do what they realize
to be best. When we say to them: Friends, you are mistaken
and are saying what is not true, they would probably reply:
Protagoras and Socrates, if this event is not to be called "being
overcome by pleasure," pray tell us what it is, and what you
would call it.

But why, Socrates, need we investigate the opinion of the
many, who just say anything that comes to their head?

I believe, I said, that they may be of use in helping us to
discover how courage is related to the other parts of virtue.
If you are disposed to abide by our agreement that I should
show the way in which, as I think, our recent difficulty is
most likely to be cleared up, do you follow. But if not, never
mind.

You are quite right, he said; and I would have you proceed as you have begun.

Well then, I said, let me suppose that they repeat their
question: What account do you give of that which, in our
way of speaking, is termed "being overcome by pleasure"? I
should answer thus: Listen, and Protagoras and I will endeavor to show you. When men are overcome by eating and
drinking and sexual desires which are pleasant, and they,
knowing them to be evil, nevertheless indulge in them, would
you not say that they were overcome by pleasure? They will
not deny this. And suppose that you and I were to go on and
ask them again: "In what way do you say that they are evil—
in that they are pleasant and give pleasure at the moment,
or because they cause disease and poverty and other like evils
in the future? Would they still be evil if they simply gave

pleasure and had no attendant evil consequences, regardless of the source and nature of the pleasure they gave?" Would they not answer, Protagoras, that they are not evil on account of the pleasure of the moment which they give, but on account of the aftereffects—diseases and the like?

e

I believe, said Protagoras, that the world in general would answer as you do.

And in causing diseases do they not cause pain? And in causing poverty do they not cause pain? They would agree to that also, if I am not mistaken?

Protagoras assented.

Then I should say to them, in my name and yours: Do you think them evil for any other reason, except because they end in pain and rob us of other pleasures? There again would they agree.

We both of us thought that they would.

354

And then we should take the question from the opposite point of view and say: "Friends, when you speak of goods being painful, do you not mean remedial goods, such as gymnastic exercises, and military service, and the physician's use of burning, cutting, drugging, and starving? Are these the things which are good but painful?"—they would assent to me?

He agreed.

And do you call them good because they occasion the greatest immediate suffering and pain; or because, afterward, they bring health and physical well-being and the salvation of the state and power over others and wealth?—they would agree to the latter alternative, if I am not mistaken?

b

utility

He assented.

Are these things good for any other reason except that they end in pleasure and get rid of and avert pain? Are you looking to any other standard but pleasure and pain when you call them good?—they would acknowledge that they were not?

c

I think so, said Protagoras.

And do you not pursue pleasure as a good, and avoid pain as an evil?

He assented.

Then you think that pain is an evil and pleasure is a good; and even pleasure you deem an evil, when it robs you of greater pleasures than it gives, or causes pains greater than d the pleasure. If, however, you call pleasure an evil in relation to some other end or standard, you will be able to show us that standard. But you have none to show.

I do not think that they have, said Protagoras.

And again, have you not a similar way of speaking about pain? You call pain a good when it takes away greater pains than those which it has, or gives pleasures greater than the pains—then, if you have some standard other than pleasure and pain to which you refer when you call actual pain a good, e you can show us what that is. But you cannot.

True, said Protagoras.

Suppose again, I said, that the world says to me, to what purpose do you spend many words and speak in many ways on this subject? Excuse me, friends, I should reply; but in the first place it is not easy to explain what that is which you call "being overcome by pleasure"; and the whole argument turns upon this. And even now, if you see any possible 355 way in which evil can be explained as other than pain, or good as other than pleasure, you may still retract. Are you satisfied, then, at having a life of pleasure which is without pain? If you are, and if you are unable to show any good or evil which does not end in pleasure and pain, hear the consequences. If what you say is true, then the statement is absurd which affirms that a man often does evil knowingly when he might abstain, because he is seduced and overpowered by b pleasure; or again, when you say that a man knowingly refuses to do what is good because he is overcome by pleasure of the moment. And that this is ridiculous will be evident if only we give up the use of various names, such as pleasant and painful, and good and evil. As there are two things, let us call them by two names—first, good and evil, and then c pleasant and painful. Assuming this, let us go on to say that a man does evil knowing that he does evil. But someone will

ask, Why? Because he is overcome, is the first answer. And by
what is he overcome? the inquirer will proceed to ask. And
we shall no longer be able to reply, "by pleasure"; for the
name of pleasure has been exchanged for that of good. In our
answer, then, we shall only say that he is overcome. By what?
he will reiterate. By the good, we shall have to reply; indeed,
we shall. Nay, but our questioner will rejoin with a laugh,
if he be one of the swaggering sort. That is too ridiculous,   d
that a man should do what he knows to be evil when he ought
not, because he is overcome by good. Is that, he will ask, because the good was worthy or not worthy of conquering the
evil? And in answer to that we shall obviously reply, Because
it was not worthy, for if it had been worthy, then he who, as
we say, was overcome by pleasure, would not have been wrong.
But how, he will reply, can the good be unworthy of the evil,
or the evil of the good? Is not the real explanation that they
are out of proportion to one another, either as greater and
smaller, or more and fewer? This we cannot deny. And when   e
you speak of being overcome, What do you mean, he will
say, but that you choose the greater evil in exchange for the
lesser good? Admitted. And now let us substitute the names of
pleasure and pain for good and evil, and say, not as before,
that a man does what is evil knowingly, but that he does what
is painful knowingly, and because he is overcome by pleasure,
which is unworthy to overcome. Are there any circumstances   356
in which pleasure is inferior to pain other than when there is
an excess and defect in their mutual relation, which means
that they become greater and smaller, and more and fewer,
and differ in degree? For if anyone says, Yes, Socrates, but the
pleasure of the moment differs widely from future pleasure
and pain, to that I should reply: And do they differ in anything but in pleasure and pain? There is nothing else. And do
you, like a skillful weigher, put in the balance the pleasures   b
and the pains, and their nearness and distance, and weigh
them, and then say which outweighs the other? If you weigh
pleasures against pleasures, you of course should take the
more and greater; or if you weigh pains against pains, you

should take the fewer and the less; or if pleasures against pains, then that course of action should be taken in which the painful is exceeded by the pleasant, whether the distant by the near or the near by the distant; and you should avoid that

c   course of action in which the pleasant is exceeded by the painful. Would you not admit, my friends, that this is true? I know that they cannot deny this.

He agreed with me.

Well then, I shall say, if you agree so far, be so good as to answer me a question: Do not objects of the same size appear larger to your sight when near, and smaller when at a distance? They will acknowledge that. And the same holds of thickness and number; also sounds, which are in themselves equal, are greater when near, and lesser when at a distance. They will grant that also. Now suppose doing well to consist

d   in doing or choosing the greater, and in not doing or in avoiding the less, what would be the saving principle of human life? Would it be the art of measuring or the power of appearance? Is not the latter that deceiving art which makes us wander up and down and take at one time the things of which we repent at another, both in our actions and in our choice of things great and small? But the art of measurement would invalidate the power of appearance and, showing the

e   truth, would fain teach the soul at last to find lasting rest in the truth, and would thus save our life. Would not mankind generally acknowledge that the art which accomplishes this result is the art of measurement?

Yes, he said, the art of measurement.

Suppose again, the salvation of human life to depend on the choice of odd and even, and on the knowledge of when a man ought to choose the greater or less, either in reference to the same quantity or to another, and whether near or at a distance. What would be the principle that makes for the salva-

357   tion of our lives? Would not knowledge—a knowledge of measuring, since this is the art that has to do with excess and defect, and a knowledge of number, when the question is of odd and even? The world will assent, will they not?

Protagoras himself thought that they would.

Well then, my friends, I say to them, seeing that the salvation of human life has been found to consist in the right choice of pleasures and pains, in the choice of the more and the fewer, and the greater and the less, and the nearer and remoter, must not this measuring be a consideration of their excess and defect and equality in relation to each other?

This is undeniably true.

And this, as possessing measure, must undeniably also be an art and science?

They will agree, he said.

The nature of this art or science will be a matter of future consideration; but the demonstration *that* it is a science has been adequately made, and that is what you asked of me and Protagoras. At the time when you asked the question, if you remember, both of us were agreeing that there was nothing mightier than knowledge, and that knowledge, in whatever existing, must prevail over pleasure and all other things. And then you said that pleasure often prevailed even over a man who has knowledge. And we refused to allow this, and you rejoined: O Protagoras and Socrates, what is the meaning of being overcome by pleasure if not this? Tell us what you call such an event? If we had immediately and at the time answered, "ignorance," you would have laughed at us. But now, in laughing at us, you will be laughing at yourselves, for you also admitted that men err in their choice of pleasures and pains, that is, in their choice of good and evil, from defect of knowledge. And you admitted further that they err, not only from defect of knowledge in general, but of that particular knowledge which, as you also agreed earlier in the discussion, is called measuring. And you are also aware that the erring act which is done without knowledge is done in ignorance. This, therefore, is the meaning of being overcome by pleasure—ignorance, and that the greatest. And our friends Protagoras and Prodicus and Hippias declare that they are the physicians of ignorance; but you, who are under the mistaken impression that ignorance is not the cause, and that the art of which I am speaking cannot be taught, neither go yourselves, nor send your children to the Sophists, who are the teachers of these things; you are concerned about your money and give them none; and the result is that you are the worse off both in public and private life. Let us suppose this to be our answer to the world in general. And now I should like to ask you, Hippias, and you, Prodicus, as well as Protagoras (for the argument is to be yours as well as ours), whether you think that I am speaking the truth or not?

They all thought that what I said was entirely true.

Then you agree, I said, that the pleasant is the good, and the painful evil. And here I would beg my friend Prodicus not to introduce his distinction of names, whether he is disposed to say pleasurable, delightful, joyful. However, by whatever name he prefers to call them, I will ask you, most excellent Prodicus, to answer in my sense of the words.

Prodicus laughed and assented, as did the others.

Then, my friends, what do you say to this? Are not all actions noble of which the tendency is to make life painless and pleasant? And the noble work is also useful and good?

This was admitted.

Then, I said, if the pleasant is the good, nobody does anything under the idea or conviction that some other thing would be better and is also attainable, when he might do the better. And this inferiority of a man to himself is merely ignorance, as the superiority of a man to himself is wisdom.

They all assented.

And is not ignorance the having a false opinion and being deceived about important matters?

To this also they unanimously assented.

Then, I said, no man voluntarily pursues evil, or that which he thinks to be evil. To pursue what one believes to be evil rather than what is good is not in human nature; and when a man is compelled to choose one of two evils, no one will choose the greater when he may have the less.

All of them agreed to every word of this.

(c) Wisdom is Courage (358d–360e)

Well, I said, there is a certain thing called fear or terror; and here, Prodicus, I should particularly like to know whether you would agree with me in defining this fear or terror as expectation of evil.

Protagoras and Hippias agreed to this definition, but Prodicus said that this was fear and not terror.

Never mind, Prodicus, I said; but let me ask whether, if   e our former assertions are true, a man will pursue that which he fears when it is open to him to pursue what he does not fear? Would not this be in flat contradiction to the admission which has been already made, that he thinks the things which he fears to be evil, and no one will pursue or voluntarily accept that which he thinks to be evil?

That also was universally admitted.   359

Then, I said, these, Hippias and Prodicus, are our premises. And I would beg Protagoras to explain to us how he can be right in what he said at first. I do not mean in what he said quite at first, for his first statement, as you may remember, was that whereas there were five parts of virtue, none of them was like any other of them; each of them had a separate function. To this, however, I am not referring, but to the assertion which he afterwards made, that of the five virtues four were nearly akin to each other, but that the fifth, which was courage, differed greatly from the others. And of   b this he gave me the following proof. He said: You will find, Socrates, that some of the most impious and unrighteous and self-indulgent and ignorant men are among the most courageous, which proves that courage is very different from the other parts of virtue. I was surprised at his saying this at the time, and I am still more surprised now that I have discussed the matter with you. So I asked him whether by the brave he meant the confident. Yes, he replied, and the aggressive. (You may remember, Protagoras, that this was your answer.)   c

He assented.

Well then, I said, tell us against what are the brave ready to go—against the same things as the cowards?

No, he answered.

Then against something different?

Yes, he said.

Then do cowards go where there is nothing to fear, and the brave where there is much to fear?

Yes, Socrates, so men say.

Very true, I said. But I want to know against what do

d you say that the brave are ready to go—against fearful things, believing them to be fearful things, or against things which are not fearful?

No, said he; the former case has been proved by you in the previous argument to be impossible.

That again, I replied, is quite true. And if this has been rightly proved, then no one goes to meet what he thinks fearful, since inferiority to oneself has been shown to be ignorance.

He assented.

And yet the brave man and the coward alike go to meet that about which they are confident; so that, in this point of

e view, the cowardly and the brave go to meet the same things.

And yet, Socrates, said Protagoras, that against which the coward goes is the opposite of that against which the brave goes. The one, for example, is willing to go to battle, and the other is not willing.

And is going to battle noble or disgraceful? I said.

Noble, he replied.

And if noble, then already admitted by us to be good; for all noble actions we have admitted to be good.

That is true; and to that opinion I shall always adhere.

True, I said. But which of the two are they who, as you

360 say, are unwilling to go to war, which is a good and noble thing?

The cowards, he replied.

And what is good and noble, I said, is also pleasant?

It has certainly been acknowledged to be so, he replied.

And do the cowards knowingly refuse to go to the nobler, and pleasanter, and better?

The admission of that, he replied, would belie our former admissions.

But does not the brave man also go to meet the better, and pleasanter, and nobler?

That must be admitted.

And the brave man has no base fear or base confidence?   b

True, he replied.

And if not base, then noble?

He admitted this.

And if noble, then good?

Yes.

But the fear and confidence of the coward or foolhardy or madman, on the contrary, are base?

He assented.

And these base and evil fears and confidence originate in ignorance and lack of learning?

True, he said.

Then as to that because of which cowards are cowards, do   c
you call it cowardice or courage?

I should say cowardice, he replied.

And have they not been shown to be cowards through their ignorance of dangers?

Assuredly, he said.

And because of that ignorance they are cowards?

He assented.

And that because of which they are cowards is admitted by you to be cowardice?

He again assented.

Then the ignorance of what is and is not fearful is cowardice?

He nodded assent.

But surely courage, I said, is opposed to cowardice?

Yes.   d

Then the wisdom which knows what are and are not fearful things is opposed to the ignorance of them?

To that again he nodded assent.

And the ignorance of them is cowardice?

To that he very reluctantly nodded assent.

And the knowledge of that which is and is not fearful is courage, and is opposed to the ignorance of these things?

At this point he would no longer nod assent, but was silent.

And why, I said, do you neither assent or dissent, Protagoras?

Finish the argument by yourself, he said.

e   I only want to ask one more question, I said. I want to know whether you still think that there are men who are most ignorant and yet most courageous?

It is contentious of you, Socrates, to make me answer. Very well, then, I will gratify you, and say that this appears to me to be impossible consistently with the argument.

9. Inconclusive Conclusion (360e–362a)

My only object, I said, in continuing with my questions has been the desire to ascertain facts about virtue and what

361   virtue itself is. For if this were clear, I am very sure that the other controversy which has been carried on at great length by both of us—you affirming and I denying that virtue can be taught—would also become clear. The result of our discussion appears to me to be singular. For if the argument had a human voice, that voice would be heard laughing at us and charging us: "Socrates and Protagoras, you are strange beings; there are you, Socrates, who were saying earlier that virtue cannot be taught, contradicting yourself now by your attempt

b   to prove that all things are knowledge, including justice, and self-control, and courage—which tends to show that virtue can certainly be taught; for if virtue were other than knowledge, as Protagoras attempted to prove, then clearly virtue cannot be taught; but if virtue is entirely knowledge, as you are seeking to show, Socrates, then I cannot but suppose that virtue is capable of being taught. Protagoras, on the other hand,

who then hypothesized that it could be taught, is now eager to
prove it to be anything rather than knowledge; and if this is
true, it must be quite incapable of being taught." Now I, Protagoras, perceiving this terrible confusion, have a great desire
that it should be cleared up. And I should like to carry on the
discussion until we finally ascertain what virtue is, and to investigate whether it is capable of being taught or not, lest
haply Epimetheus should trip us up and deceive us in the
argument, as he forgot us in the story. Even as you were telling the myth, I preferred your Prometheus to your Epimetheus, for of him I make constant use, whenever I am busy
about these questions, in Promethean care of my own life in
its entirety. And if you have no objection, as I said at first,
I should like to have your help in the inquiry.

Protagoras replied: Socrates, I am not of a base nature,
and I am the last man in the world to be envious. I cannot
but applaud your energy and your conduct of an argument.
As I have often said, I admire you above all the men I
meet, and far above all men of your age; and I dare say that
I would not be surprised if you were to become one of those
who are distinguished for their wisdom. Let us come back to
the subject at some future time of your choice; at present we
had better turn to something else.

By all means, I said, if that is your wish; for I too ought
long since to have kept the engagement of which I spoke before, and only tarried because I could not refuse the request
of the noble Callias. So the conversation ended, and we went
our way.